FINANCIAL WARFARE

Also by Yvonne Brooks

Daily Financial Journal

Financial Confessions

Visu-Finance Bible Study Series

Visu-Success Pre-Teen Plan

Kids Finance 101

Financial Planning for Teens

100 Ways to Become a Successful Teenager

FINANCIAL WARFARE

How To Fight and Win

YVONNE BROOKS

iUniverse, Inc.
New York   Bloomington   Shanghai

Financial Warfare
How To Fight and Win

Copyright © 2008 by Yvonne Brooks

iUniverse books may be ordered through booksellers or by contacting:

iUniverse
1663 Liberty Drive
Bloomington, IN 47403
www.iuniverse.com
1-800-Authors (1-800-288-4677)

Because of the dynamic nature of the Internet, any Web addresses or links contained in this book may have changed since publication and may no longer be valid.

ISBN: 978-0-595-51892-0 (pbk)
ISBN: 978-0-595-62077-7 (ebk)

Printed in the United States of America

The information, ideas, and suggestions in this book are not intended to render professional advice. Before following any suggestions contained in this book, you should consult your personal accountant or other financial advisor. Neither the author nor the publisher shall be liable or responsible for any loss or damage allegedly arising as a consequence of your use or application of any information or suggestions in this book.

Spiritual Leadership Series

Yes, I'm on my way to visit you with judgment. I'll present compelling evidence against sorcerers, adulterers, liars, those who exploit workers, those who take advantage of widows and orphans, those who are inhospitable to the homeless-anyone and everyone who doesn't honor me. A Message from God-of-the-Angel-Armies.

Malachi 3:5

Dedication to Mentors:

Many thanks to my spiritual and financial mentors;

Your sermons, prayers, seminars, writings and books helped to give me the confidence mandatory to successfully complete the book *Financial Warfare*.

After reading and listening to several hundred copies of your books and tapes; I was convinced that you were all sent to me for such a time as this.

Thank you all for being mighty warriors in this financial war. Your victories in the past laid the foundation for many. In addition, my own victory in this financial war is a testimony that you are still bringing glory to God.

May God bless you all richly according to Deuteronomy 1:11

O Father, Lord of heaven and earth, thank you for hiding these things from those who think themselves wise and clever, and for revealing them to the childlike. Yes, Father, it pleased you to do it this way.

Luke 10:21

Contents

The world is unprincipled. It's dog-eat-dog out there! The world doesn't fight fair. But we don't live or fight our battles that way-never have and never will.

2 Corinthians 10:3

My Testimony

A simple definition of war in the natural world is an act of force intended to compel the opponent to fulfill our will. When a person is in a financial war, the life-style of the entire family is affected. Outstanding financial debt, and low paying jobs often force many to comply with the demands of poverty. Parents spend hours working two or three jobs trying to keep up with the cost of rising inflation.

Family members are usually alerted to this invasion by constant arguments and battles in their home about never having enough money. Financial instability is often increased due to lack of financial education, and divorce is always at the root for the majority of families who get wounded badly during this war.

My first exposure to this war happened to me as a child. I watched closely as both my parents suffered greatly financially. As I got older, I watched as other family members and friends were being torn apart due to compelling thoughts and worries about the lack of money.

It was after years of losing my own personal financial battle that God gave me the assignment of writing this book *"Financial Warfare"*. To be honest, my first reaction was not good. I petitioned with God about all my financial troubles and proceeded to explain to him about my lack of qualifications as an effective writer. I also reminded God that I was labeled to be a trouble maker and voted "most rebellious child" by family members and the churches I attended.

After I was finished disqualifying myself, God said "You're perfect for the job!" Now I was in trouble! It did not matter to God what other people thought about me. God knew me before the foundation of the earth and did not need a resume.

The book title alone sent fear all through my body. I dare not share this assignment with friends or family members. How could I? I was presently in a financial war and losing every battle. Attackers had me under surveillance with a hose attached securely to my wallet, getting ready for the kill. I was about to lose everything.

The first chapter took about ten months. The journey began early one morning when I was awakened by the Holy Spirit at a time when no one would consider waking up. My first assignment was to take notes and wait **confidently** for the next assignment. This made no sense to me. I had no idea how to wait with confidence.

My second assignment was exciting, but at the same time scary. The first chapter that came to me was the chapters on "The Attack-Dirty Financial Secrets Exposed!" These chapters took over a year to write. Now, I knew for sure I was heading in a direction where I was definitely not qualified. I needed a lot of time to process how the new revelations could change my own financial situation. So, I took a break from writing. I had convinced myself that this assignment was too hard and too heavy. To which God reminded me that the sub-title of the book was "How to Fight and Win, not how to fight and lose."

Well, while praying one morning, I was complaining about my bills, again! I asked God where was the wealth and riches that he had showed me in my visions? In a soft, kind, and quiet voice he replied "It's on your computer." I started laughing hysterically. My laughter turned into tears and soon after, a beautiful spirit entered my home bringing comfort and guidance. I no longer felt inadequate. This was my first time experiencing the joy of the scripture *"Greater is he that is in me, than he that is in the world."*

Each chapter of my writings reflected where I was financially. Every chapter directed me to another mentor, more research, more fasting, more prayer, planting a series of financial seeds and at times complete isolation from friends and family. People were taken out my life for reasons I later found out for my protection, and based upon the number of people that were taken; I needed allot of protection. How great is our God!

Some days I received one word, other days I received a couple of sentences. Whatever and whenever God spoke, I became a willing vessel to this awesome assignment. Just reading each chapter over and over again brought new insight and ideas to change my limited thinking from establishing one saving account to multiple streams of savings. The *"Financial Warfare"* book project was now exciting.

Excitement was pushing me closer and closer towards a quick finish of the book. However, I was mistaken. I was instructed by the Holy Spirit to **rewrite** each chapter with new discernment and anointing. I was then instructed to read Isaiah 45 and the book of Ezra to prepare properly to receive the Cyrus anointing. It was not a happy moment, but I wanted to try. Actually, it was easier to write with my new insights and powerful anointing. I enjoyed writing, finally! I felt empowered to write with more enthusiasm and confidence. I became bold and knew without a doubt that I could write with greatness. It was a way to draw even closer to God. What a wonderful God we serve!

The release of *"Financial Warfare"* was a heavy burden to carry. It taught me how to be still and know that God is always with me. I also felt that writing this book was not only for me. I felt that others would be set free to experience and enjoy God's blessings, simply by reading each chapter.

It does not matter what financial level you may be at. It does not matter if you are currently financially illiterate and unemployed. God's economic principles will work for anyone with a willing heart to become productive for the Glory of God. If God can use me to speak life into your financial situation; he can use you to bring success and Glory to his name.

Release came for me when I began implementing God's secrets about financial independence one at a time. I started by changing my thoughts about God's money. I gave God thanks for my current situation and started to sow financial seeds weekly to family members, friends, and my community. I also embraced financial scriptures and spoke them over each situation.

Eventually I began applying God's economic strategies against every financial stronghold that I was in bondage to, which changed my whole life. It was a call to be fully armed. Never again will I allow strongholds to seduce or keep me in financial bondage. Never again will I believe the lies being told by false prophets that becoming a Christian means living in poverty. I am a child of the King, and God has given me the power to create great wealth to bring Glory to his Name!

I am no longer a victim to the things of this world. You are no longer powerless to strongholds. Together we have more than enough power to change the financial atmosphere in our homes and communities by choosing to be financially responsible with income, savings and investments for God's Glory. We are more than conquerors; therefore we no longer fight without definite aim. We are fully aware of the enemy and subdue every financial stronghold successfully through Jesus Christ. No exception!

Christ is the visible image of the Invisible God. He existed before anything was created and is supreme over all creation, for through him God created everything in the heavenly realms and on earth. He made the things we can see and the things we can't see-such as thrones, kingdoms, rulers, and authorities in the unseen world. Everything was created through him and for him.

Colossians 1:15,16

Chapter One

The Invisible War

Chapter One: The Invisible War
Ladies and gentleman, wake up! We are under attack!

There is a great invisible war being waged globally against the children of God and it is called financial warfare. This invisible war respects no one and is gaining new ground every second. What is financial warfare and what does it mean to fight and win?

Financial Warfare is an invisible war fought both in the spiritual and physical realms against children of God and demonic forces settled in high places.

One of the greatest wars that you will ever fight in your lifetime on planet earth is this invisible financial war. The physical reality of your financial situation today is a direct reflection of your ability to fight victoriously or not.

The inability to see this invisible financial war means that your financial situation is already in complete darkness. Bounced checks, excess fees for late payments and a series of inflated interest rates will follow for generations due to your inability to see what dirty tricks and nasty fighting techniques are being used to attack your financial resurrection.

In every aspect of your life you can expect to be attacked, assaulted and financially pillaged. Just look around your own household, your neighborhood, your community, your state, your country and the world. Many have eyes, but do not see!

Indeed, much of this financial warfare is beyond your ability to see and influence except through learning how to use visible and invisible financial weaponry given to you thousands of years ago through Jesus Christ.

Whether you believe that you are in a financial war or not, do not matter at this point. Financial warfare exists and takes casualties on a daily basis with or without your insight. If you are still unconvinced, check out the obituaries and divorce courts and consider why so many men commit suicide or leave their families as head of their household. Could it be because of an invisible war that they refused to recognize?

God's economic principle is the most devalued attribute for those who are blinded to financial warfare. There seems to be an alarming amount of people throughout the world who are defeated and left for dead because they refused to accept God's Word as the perfect firearm against financial strongholds. You must wage ruthless and continuous war against every destructive financial choice you make that keep you in bondage.

Thoughts and ideas about poverty can be great enemies during financial warfare. Negative thoughts about money and wealth often release an economic condition into the lives of many that later cause lack of both money and basic necessities needed to live successfully such as; food, water, education and shelter.

Without Financial Education, Something Terrible Happens, DEBT!

Stay alert! Watch out for your great enemy, the devil. He prowls around like a roaring lion, looking for someone to devour. ***1 Peter 5:8***

It is abnormal to have the ability to earn income, yet be plagued by generational debt. God's financial weaponry is a necessary ingredient to fight this invisible war successfully.

Constant manipulations and suggestions about lack of money are being used over and over as a weapon to attack the uneducated and those who believe that God wants them to be poor.

The cycle of poverty is an attack perpetuated by thoughts, ideas, and suggestions about lack! This attack is constantly recurring for individuals who refuse to welcome God's economic wisdom.

Lack is a state of needing something that is absent or unavailable. Believing that you have unlimited access to financial resources is the key. In God all your needs are met. Therefore it is a contradiction to say that you believe God provides while at the same time experiencing lack.

Can your lack help those in need? Can your inability to pay your bills bring a lost soul to God? How does lack of financial increase in your life help the homeless and those who believe in poverty? Thoughts and ideas that support lack go against the will of God. It is evil to think that God wants **his** children to be poor.

Due to an individual's lack of financial education, he or she at times become blinded to compounded interest saving programs, and find it difficult to establish multiple streams of savings accounts before graduating high school.

It is amazing to see what our negative thoughts and ideas about money have created upon the earth. Jesus Christ died on the cross so that those who confess with their mouth, that he died and rose from the dead for their sins would receive authority to take dominion over everything on the earth. This includes wealth and riches.

How is it that you have come to believe the lie that you should worship your enemies: "poverty" and "lack?" Why are God's children so obsessed with living a lifestyle that supports the flesh?

Are you delusional enough to believe that this invisible financial war is not real because you cannot see it with your naked eyes?

Many churches collect four to five offerings at each gathering, yet refuse to establish programs that teach their congregation how to increase their income, balance their checkbooks or how to stay away from financial devourers such as credit cards and loan companies who charge outrageous interest fees.

Don't under estimate the enemy. God's children must declare war **immediately** against all thoughts, ideas and suggestions that come against God's economic plan. The only way to take economic dominion is to submit all thoughts and ideas to the Lord at the beginning of each day.

The Lord replies, "I have seen violence done to the helpless, and I have heard the groans of the poor. Now I will rise up to rescue them, as they have longed for me to do."

Psalms 12:5

God has provided unlimited financial wisdom in the Bible for you to gain wealth. God's economic wisdom is available to everyone. God does not discriminate.

There are libraries in every community with books written by authors from a wide variety of financial backgrounds waiting to share their knowledge with you at no cost. There are bookstores, schools and professionals who offer ideas in their seminars on how to gain more wealth and eliminate debt. There is no lack—in God.

It is heart wrenching to see the sufferings of those who consider themselves to be the working poor. Most families work over 60 hours or more weekly only to have more debt and less-savings due to immature spending.

There are studies now in America that shows children going to bed hungry due to lack of support or funds in families where parents are employed. How can this be possible if you believe in a God with infinite riches?

- Why are you afraid of poverty and lack?
- Why is poverty such a constant headache for God's children?
- Why are so many Christians in debt?
- What bible are you reading?
- How can you use the Word of God to confront financial issues that has controlled you for decades?
- Why do you allow your finances and hard work to be attacked by invisible demonic forces?
- When will you stop playing the victim and become financially victorious for Christ?

Commercials (a successful weapon used by financial strongholds-covered in chapter four) have become the perfect seducers to set the stage for a financial rape to take place. Please understand that this act of rape is premeditated. Advertisers spend billions of dollars just to find out the secrets of their target audience.

Corporations calculate and run test after test to set the stage for financial foreplay. Financial foreplay is the first step needed to make sure that each victim is truly intoxicated and saturated with countless advertisements. Once completely intoxicated, consumers will open their wallets and do whatever it takes to get credit, only to say "**YES**" to another purchase.

God's children should learn about invisible and visible financial weaponry by increasing their vision, diligence and wisdom. Don't look for others to bail you out of debt. Develop God's economic principles for yourself by eliminating greed, deceit, laziness and rebellion. See with your own eyes that you have the ability to win this invisible financial war successfully. There is only first place in this financial war. Second place is not acceptable. Use your fighting skills with confidence!

But people who aren't spiritual can't receive these truths from God's Spirit. It all sounds foolish to them and they can't understand it, for only those who are spiritual can understand what the Spirit means. Those who are spiritual can evaluate all things, but they themselves cannot be evaluated by others. **1 Corinthians 2:14,15**

LACK OF FINANCIAL VISION is a sign to investigate to see if you have welcomed a demonic force into your finances. Your financial success is based upon your ability to see in the spirit where God has stationed you to be financially.

If you are unable to see clearly where you are heading financially, it is very safe to say that your financial war is at a critical point. Read this book carefully.

God has already given you many financial dreams and visions. What have you done with them? What will you tell God when he asks for a report on all the financial visions that he gave you? Did you build the hospital God whispered to you about years ago? Did you send money to the orphans God put you in charge of? Did you build those homes for the needy? Did you write that book he placed upon your heart?

Increased financial visions are crucial if you are to maximize the resources God has entrusted to you. Where do you see yourself financially in the next twenty years? What are some of the financial visions that God gave you in secret? When was the last time you sat down and wrote out or reviewed your five-year financial plan?

Possible attributes of a person who lack financial vision may include the following:

- Refusing to write down financial goals.
- Take financial advice from a lazy person.
- Spend more time watching TV and less time studying the Word.
- Has the answer to everyone's problem, just not their own.
- Inconsistent with assignments and relationships.
- Procrastinate (I will do it tomorrow, next week, never!)

A clear financial vision will help to develop an accurate picture of your access to unlimited opportunities waiting for you, just for the taking. Once your financial vision is clear, take the time to commit your plans to God and receive direct access to increase.

Examples of a successful financial vision plan may include:

1. See yourself as a channel of abundance for blessing others.
2. See yourself financially responsible with your family and your community.
3. See yourself lacking nothing; therefore all your needs are met.

Do not be a know it all. Be patient, take your time; seek counsel from heaven. There is only one of you on this planet. God had you in mind when he thought of many ways to display his greatness. God loves expressing his short and long term goals through you. God is a visionary and so are all those who trust and believe in him.

Commit your actions to the Lord, and your plans will succeed. **Proverbs 16:3**

LACK OF FINANCIAL WISDOM is another reason why so many fail their financial wars. Lack of financial wisdom produces instability and poverty. It is impossible to achieve financial success without wisdom.

Increased financial wisdom is the ability to understand the inner qualities and language of money. Financial wisdom is financial intelligence. The ability to understand and articulate daily financial teachings into prosperity will take wisdom.

What is your understanding about money? How does money work for you? Is money working for you? What is your current net-worth? What is your credit score? Do you understand how compound interests works? How much income have you earned within the past ten years? Do you have a record as to how that money was spent? These are questions you should ask yourself to get a better insight about the reasons for past financial failures or success.

You must first evaluate your past relationship with money before seeking financial increase. Evaluating your relationship with money will give insights about where you need to make changes and when to seek counsel for guidance. Money is not evil once you've achieved financial wisdom. However, lack of financial wisdom can produce a negative feeling that money is evil; due to one's inability to manage current income successfully. Some questions to ponder would be:

1. Why do you spend more than you earn?
2. Why are you in debt?
3. At what age did you begin your pursuit for financial education?
4. Who are your financial mentors?

Have you noticed the lack of financial education being taught to children? Daily financial decisions are based upon financial education received from elementary school until the present moment. Your ability to make good or poor financial decisions is a result of past financial education. Not the devil.

Take inventory about the amount of financial education you have received in the past; then take a look at your financial portfolio; it should be a perfect match. Individuals who include financial education as a part of their daily ritual have more savings than those who have no interest to learn how money can be used to honor God.

Your financial assignment daily is to increase your worth. It is not to produce debt. Learn to value financial information. Plan ahead by using the financial wisdom learned in this book to establish financial independence for your household today.

Create a plan to solve financial issues before late fees begin to attach themselves to your account. Become wise with your spending. You do not need to stand in line for hours on "Black Friday" to use your savings to purchase items you do not need. Stay alert before these schemes destroy your home.

My people are ruined because they don't known what's right or true. **Proverbs 4:6**

LACK OF FINANCIAL DILIGENCE is one of the reasons why so many of God's children are attracted to poverty. The inability to stick to your financial plans until it produces success is due to a lack of diligence. Lack of financial diligence means you give up easily on your financial goals.

Many work hard to save their money only to have an emergency take their savings. An individual in this situation without diligence would give up and begin to entertain thoughts of lack. However, thoughts of lack have friends such as hopelessness, depression and failure.

Individuals who practice emotional spending are those who feel that they are incapable of acquiring success with their current financial increase. Emotional spending is wasting money due to feelings of loneliness, sadness, rejection, depression and or suspicion.

Train yourself to be peaceful around money. Put $100 in your wallet and do not spend it for one-year. If $100 is too high, use a smaller denomination until you break the anxiety and destructive feelings towards money. Be strong and reject the quick fix strategy of spending without a plan. It does not work.

Lack of financial diligence has caused many to develop out of control spending habits. God encourages his children to sit down and count the cost first before proceeding with all assignments. You must recognize attributes in yourself that attract financial destruction and constant failure. God wants you to succeed, so lift your head high and think like a successful warrior, not a captured slave.

How can one break the cycle of poverty and acquire financial diligence? Increase financial diligence is simply taking attentive care with each financial goal. Striving for excellence is the desire of one who has acquired financial diligence. There are unlimited ways to develop persistence with your financial goals. Remember, this will take time, effort and patience.

Attributes of an individual with financial diligence may include:

- Self-discipline
- Think long term
- Never give up
- Able to see the big picture
- Learn from mistakes
- Limit interruptions
- Stay focused
- Patience

The diligent find freedom in their work; the lazy are oppressed by work.

Proverbs 12:24

LAZINESS is a famous attribute of those who allow demonic forces to take charge of their finances. Laziness is procrastination and a lack of desire to perform work. Demons love lazy people, so watch your response and attitude towards your job.

Some possible attributes of a lazy person may include the following:
- **Does not like to work.**
  Lazy people finally die of hunger because they won't get up and go to work. **Proverbs 21:25**
- **Loves to sleep.**
  As a door swings back and forth on its hinges, so the lazy person turns over in bed. **Proverbs 26:14**
- **Irritates their bosses.**
  A lazy employee will give you nothing but trouble; it's vinegar in the mouth, smoke in the eyes. **Proverbs 10:26**
- **Believes their own lies.**
  Lazy people consider themselves smarter than seven wise counselors. **Proverbs 26:16**
- **Is hungry during harvest.**
  Those too lazy to plow in the right season will have no food at the harvest. **Proverbs 20:4**
- **Refuses instructions.**
  Take a lesson from the ants, you lazybones. Learn from their ways and become wise. **Proverbs 6:6**
- **Gossips rather than work.**
  Work brings profit, but mere talk leaders to poverty! **Proverbs 14:23**
- **Lives in a fantasy world.**
  A hard worker has plenty of food, but a person who chases fantasies ends up in poverty. **Proverbs 28:19**
- **Is not respected.**
  Make it your goal to live a quiet life, minding your own business and working with your hands, just as we instructed you before. Then people who are not Christians will respect the way you live, and you will not need to depend on others. **1 Thessalonians 4:11,12**
- **Have no common sense.**
  I walked by the field of a lazy person, the vineyard of one with no common sense. **Proverbs 24:30**
- **Is attacked by scarcity.**
  A little extra sleep, a little more slumber, a little folding of the hands to rest—then poverty will pounce on you like a bandit; scarcity will attack you like an armed robber. **Proverbs 24:33,34**

Even while we were with you, we gave you this command. "Those unwilling to work will not get to eat." Yet we hear that some of you are living idle lives, refusing to work and meddling in other people's business. We command such people and urge them in the name of the Lord Jesus Christ to settle down and work to earn their own living.

2 Thessalonians 3:10-12

You must work to provide basic needs. No one is responsible for your financial increase or lack there of. Embrace the art of working diligently to produce income for yourself and your family without procrastination.

Lazy people believe they are entitled to all the benefits the world has to offer without contribution. Being lazy during the times of an invisible financial war will bring shame and disgrace to your family.

It is laziness that causes someone not to prepare a monthly budget that will track personal income and expenses. It is laziness that causes some of us to refuse work only because it pays minimum wage. If you are not working, minimum wage is an increase.

Laziness breeds destruction and must be dealt with forcefully. Get excited about helping others if you do not have a job. Stop taking advantage of those who work their economic plan. Get motivated about your own ability to contribute more to others daily.

Lazy people are poisonous to everyone and will never succeed. For those who are bound up by laziness, my suggestion is to refuse this defeating tactic and change your thinking to line up with the Will of God for your life. You will be glad that you did.

To be wealthy is a gift from God, not something you earn on your own. God is the author of all of our lives. God is the only one with information regarding detailed plans for you to prosper, even before you were born. It is mandatory to seek God's face for financial wisdom. He will never fail you!

Every penny that you earn belongs to God, the creator of all things. Any and all forms of personal successes belong to God. Once you understand this simple principle, your financial attacks will cease to cause a negative effect.

When you go to work and earn a paycheck, this act should be to the glory of God. The money earned is a blessing from God to provide food and shelter for your family. Learn to respect time and money. Develop good stewardship with every dollar earned and eliminate laziness.

God created you to do great work on the earth for him. These works include becoming a channel of abundance to take care of those who are bombarded in this invisible financial war with no way of escape for generations. You were created to be a good steward with God's money. Can God trust you to fight and win this war victoriously?

You know that these hands of mine have worked to supply my own needs and even the needs of those who were with me. And I have been a constant example of how you can help those in need by working hard. You should remember the words of the Lord Jesus; "It is more blessed to give than to receive." **Acts 20: 34,35**

DECEIT is a force that visits the homes of those who are not able to recognize the affects of this invisible financial war.

The spirit of deceit intentionally conceals the truth about financial situations with the intended purpose of misleading others. Your physical behavior often gives warning signals as to whether or not you have entered the demonic arena of deceit.

Possible deceitful behaviors may include:
1. Writing a check without money in the bank to cover the amount.
2. Paying only a portion of the tithe.
3. Cheating on your taxes.
4. Not counting cash received as income.
5. Stealing pens, money, toilet paper and supplies from your job.
6. Writing incorrect information on your resume.
7. Lying about your accomplishments.

Deceit is a major sign to consider because it is one of the most powerful and effective reasons why so many get to the pinnacle of their careers and loose their homes, cars and family.

Once a person allows the spirit of deceit to enter their finances, it removes the protection of God and gives permission for demonic forces to move in and take up residence that could last twenty, thirty, fifty years or more and even a life time for some of us.

The spirit of deceit works effectively by getting someone to believe something that is not true about his/her financial situation. Deceitful tactics such as; I can't afford it, I don't have enough, or there are no jobs, are all statements used by individuals who have invited the demonic spirit of deceit into their home.

Deceiving God's children is considered one of the highest areas of control by demonic forces in the invisible financial war. Financial strongholds (covered in chapter four) usually take up residence in places such as corporations, governments and industries that influence mankind and the financial world; making it harder to comprehend God's goodness.

A good example of one who is being controlled by a deceitful spirit would be someone who applies for several credit cards, convincing themselves that it is an excellent idea to borrow at a very high interest rate while making minimum payments each month.

This kind of deceit opens up a demonic door that often stays open longer than what the individual anticipated. A credit card with a balance of $2000 can multiply itself by several hundreds developing a series of anxieties and fear toward money.

Lord, you alone are my inheritance, my cup of blessing. You guard all that is mine. The land you have given me is a pleasant land. What a wonderful inheritance!

Psalm 16:5,6

The invisible financial wars cannot be seen by those who see in part. The inability to see in the spirit will often cripple credit card junkies, cause sleepless nights, chronic fatigue and sometimes even death.

It is very important that you understand clearly that the ability to see and know in the spiritual realm only comes from God. Spiritual sight is mandatory to stay successful in the world of finance. There are many ways to produce riches, but only one way to keep wealth and live in peace. The Lord Jesus Christ.

Take a good look at CEO's of major corporations who have access to unlimited wealth; due to lack of financial insight (that comes only from God), they become victims of a deceitful spirit that produces fraud, overspending and debt that passes down to their children and grandchildren.

For decades, cigarette manufactures have intentionally misled consumers by withholding evidence about secondhand smoke and the danger it can cause to our health. In addition, there are many lost lives and empty savings accounts that support the affect of deceitful tactics used by cigarette manufactures for years. This type of financial deceit can also be found in the following:

1. Lead found in toys and the effects on a child's mental development.
2. The real cost for gasoline at the pump.
3. Billions of tax dollars used for the "war on drugs."
4. Stock markets loosing money.
5. Paying someone less money than they are worth.
6. Over charging seniors for simple medications and services.
7. Predatory lenders.
8. The cost of housing

Another uprising that is causing great harm to families is financial infidelity. Financial infidelity is considered to be a major reason why so many families fall apart. There is an alarming amount of spouses today who deliberately lie to each other about their spending habits. Hiding receipts and spending thousands of dollars without the acknowledgment of your spouse is dishonest.

Honesty is very important in all successful relationships. A healthy relationship with God is the only thing on earth that guarantees unlimited prosperity and good health to enjoy riches. Peace with increased wealth and riches can be achieved only through Christ.

Be encouraged, surrender to God for guidance and protection from destructive behaviors designed to prevent you from receiving the blessings God has released for all those who receive his son Jesus Christ as their Lord and Savior.

I have told you all this so that you may have peace in me. Here on earth you will have many trials and sorrows. But take heart, because I have overcome the world.

John 16:33

GREED is distributed by invitation only to those who refuse to gain financial wisdom early in life.

Greed is a selfish desire for material wealth or gain without reason. Those motivated by greed are spiritually blind and have no idea that they are in an invisible financial war that clearly uses the opponents against themselves.

There is no justification for the amount of greed that takes place in our governments, school districts and corporations. Yet, we are bombarded daily through the media about the number of high officials who are being investigated for greed.

Greed is purely related to materialism. The next get rich scheme or the love of money can bring great temptation to many. Many are in such a rush to get rich that they forget that it is God who gives the power to create and keep wealth.

Some possible attributes of a greedy person may include the following:
- Feeling uneasy around people who are wealthy.
- Getting angry after misplacing a small amount of money.
- Giving a gift and wanting to be properly credited or thanked for it.
- Feeling relief about problems, just by going shopping.
- Complaining constantly about not having enough.

How is it, that even high officials are not aware of this invisible war? How is it that major corporations can engage in such low and detestable acts of greed that hurt millions of people?

When will you wake up to the lies being told by the oil and insurance companies about their profit margins? Why do you still believe the lies being told about the cost of health care, when doctors are receiving huge kickbacks just by referring a patient for x-rays, or for excessive drug prescriptions? Is everyone dead to this war?

Greed is due to the fact that many are caught up in an invisible financial war. You entered the battle zone when you were conceived. The foods you eat, the place you live, the clothes you wear and the gifts you give to your family and friends all cost money. No family can survive in this world without the ability to take care of themselves financially. **This world operates by money.** You have no choice but to participate.

Money is not meant to be worshipped yet many become proud, arrogant, and trust solely in their wealth. There are those who would rather work sixty to one hundred hours weekly just to keep the illusion of wealth that they have traded their family and friends for. The idea of honoring the Sabbath is a dirty word to the greedy.

Greedy Christians should stay away from check cashing and payday loan establishments; this is a devourer sent to take money away from those who do not pay their tithes. Those who are crippled by greed should ask God for help now, tomorrow is too late.

Then he said, "Beware! Guard against every kind of greed. Life is not measured by how much you own. **Luke 12:15**

REBELLION is a clear sign confirming that you are deep into the battlefield. The spirit of rebellion is a favorite amongst those who believe that they can spend whatever they please without consequences. How foolish can they be!

Individuals with the spirit of rebellion believe the money that God provided through a job; business or gifting is one hundred percent theirs to keep. No accounting is necessary when the spirit of rebellion enters their financial world.

Possible attributes of a person with the spirit of rebellion may include the following:
- Loves gambling with their life and money.
- Believes that God has nothing to do with their financial increase.
- Impatient.
- Compares themselves to others.
- Registers with every get rich quick business opportunity.
- Unreliable.
- Argumentative.

The rebellious are constantly in a rush to get it all. The rebellious want their riches right now. Fast, easy and quick. It is rebellion when you refuse to put away savings for your children's education for the future. It is rebellion when you do not pay your taxes on time.

The spirit of rebellion is effective because at times many do not want to follow the economic plan that God instructed. Many love to challenge and disobey all laws, whether they are of God or man.

The rebellious looks for every way to skip out on paying tithes and taxes. The rebellious looks for ways to hide money from God and the government. Laws are created for those who have a tendency to rebel. If you followed the law, there would be no need for the spirit of rebellion.

Bankruptcy cannot save you. Refusing to pay your bills on time will not change the fact that you are getting seriously beat up in this financial war. Time is running out.

Trust God to guide your finances!

The wise have wealth and luxury, but fools spend whatever they get.
Prov:21:20

Chapter One: Financial Warfare Summary

Invisible War:

Invisible war is a type of financial warfare fought both in the spiritual and physical realms against children of God and demonic forces settled in high places. Negative thoughts about money releases an economic condition that produces lack; so fight and win this financial war by using God's economic principles.

Lack of Financial Vision:

Lack of financial vision is the inability to see where one is heading financially short and long term. Financial visions are critical in order to maximize all the blessings God has released from heaven to you.

Lack of Financial Wisdom:

Lack of financial wisdom is the inability to understand the language of money. Your relationship with money can give insights about how money can be used as a positive force for financial increase. Win this war by expecting your assignments to produce increase from this day forth.

Lack of Financial Diligence:

Lack of financial diligence is giving up easily on financial goals. Emotional spending is the fastest way to waste money; so become financially diligent by making the most of what you already have, and create a plan for future spending before shopping.

Laziness:

Laziness is procrastination in its highest form. Demons love lazy people; so keep an eye out for attributes that encourage laziness. Work with diligence to provide your own basic needs. Become a channel of abundance for yourself, your family and your community.

Deceit:

The spirit of deceit intentionally conceals the truth about financial situations with the intended purpose of misleading others. Be encouraged and surrender to God for guidance and protection.

Greed:

Greed is a selfish desire for material wealth or gain without reason. Beware! Guard your heart against every kind of greed and allow generosity to fill your soul.

Rebellion:

The spirit of rebellion does not follow rules and regulations. Remember, those who follow the law have wealth and riches. Those who disobey the law spend all their money and later became poor.

Chapter One: Voice Activated Financial Confessions

Wealth and riches are in my home. Praise the Lord!

Because I honor the Lord with my wealth and with the best part of everything I produce. God fills my home with prosperity, and my wallet overflows with riches.

I am a tither, therefore the Lord God of Heaven's Armies will open the windows of heaven for me, and will pour out a blessing so great I won't have enough room to take it in.

I will not get tired of doing well; because at just the right time God my provider has promised that I will reap a harvest of blessing if I do not give up.

I am wealthy and my treasuries are always filled because I love the Lord.

I have favor from the Lord because I seek his face daily.

God has given me the power to create more wealth because I give freely to others.

My inheritance from the Lord will pass down to my great grandchildren.

All my plans succeed because I commit my actions to the Lord.

I listen to God's instructions so that I may prosper in all that I do.

I feed, and lend to the poor, and God has repaid me generously.

My good planning and hard work will lead me closer to prosperity.

Through the knowledge of God, my rooms are filled with all sorts of precious riches and valuables.

I lack nothing in my life because I care about the rights of the poor.

I am clothed with strength and dignity, and I laugh without fear of the future because the God of Abraham, Isaac, and Jacob is also my God.

Financial Prayer
Habakkuk 3:1-2

A prayer of the prophet Habakkuk, with orchestra:

God, I've heard what our ancestors say about you, and I'm stopped in my tracks, down on my knees. Do among us what you did among them. Work among us as you worked among them. And as you bring judgment, as you surely must, remember mercy.

No soldier when in service gets entangled in the enterprises of civilian life; his aim is to satisfy and please the one who enlisted him.

2 Timothy 2:4

Chapter Two

The Warriors Heart
(Evaluation before Training)

Chapter Two: The Warriors Heart

This chapter is designed to evaluate your ability as a warrior to cope with the intellectual, spiritual and emotional demands of the financial world in your present life.

The goal is to make sure that you understand completely what is expected of you as a financial warrior.

Exposing the warrior's heart is designed to help enlisted fighters to become more honest about their warriors abilities before advancing to the frontline. Financial suicide is no longer an option for God's children.

Do you have a warrior's heart?
* What does a warrior's heart look like?
* Is he/she at peace with personal finances?
* Does the warrior enjoy giving to others?
* What are the warrior's financial disorders?
* Do the warrior's financial decisions reflect that of a fool or from God?
* Is the warrior emotionally, intellectually and spiritually competent enough to take financial territory for the Lord?
    - For themselves?
    - For their family?
    - For their friends?
    - For their community?
* Is the warrior capable of financially supporting the body of Christ?
* Does the warrior believe the **Word** of the True Living God?
* Does the warrior know who he/she is in Christ?

A warrior's heart should be a self-corrective device designed to free the unlimited greatness God created in all his children. This would be a good time to embrace your ability to achieve financial victory in your mind, before entering the battlefield.

Your feelings about increased debt and overspending are a direct response from your thoughts and ideas about prosperity. These thoughts and ideas can either assist towards becoming financially responsible or help to perpetuate the role of a victim. Your first assignment as a fighter is to capture every thought, idea and suggestion that do not line up with God's word about your financial increase and bring them into subjection.

Becoming financially responsible on a daily basis will always put you in a position of power. There will be no desire for envy or greed when you are financially responsible.

Financially independent individuals understand that whatever financial state they are in at the present moment began with their thoughts of increase or lack; not because of someone else. Financially independent individuals know that God will always show them a way out of all financial adversity.

Chapter two exposes each warrior's weaknesses and strengths. Your answers to the warrior's evaluation will give a better understanding of what negative ideas and suggestions you are allowing to enter through your ears and eyes gate; receptors used in this battle to produce victory or defeat.

Whatever you allow through the ears and eyes gate will eventually make its way to your heart. Once your heart is full of good or bad thoughts about your financial situation, the mouth will begin to speak and bear fruit according to the abundance of the heart.

<u>Some ways to protect your ears and eyes gate may include:</u>
- Limit the amount of negative information received about money.
- Read books that encourage saving and investing.
- Stay away from people who complain about paying their bills.
- Refuse to listen to people who will not work to take care of their own needs.
- Read and listen to the Word of God daily.
- Keep a prayer journal and write financial prayers to God.

By completing the questionnaire in this chapter, you will have a more realistic grasp of where you stand before advancing to the frontline. Be encouraged, you have the ability to overcome and experience wealth infinitely. The same power that raised Jesus from the dead lives in you and is ready to carry you towards financial victory. Your financial victory is waiting for you! Be strong, God is on your side.

Please do not read ahead to chapter three. It could be very dangerous. Complete your evaluation first. This will prepare your mind properly and ensure your ability to fight this war and win with confidence.

A good person produces good things from the treasury of a good heart, and an evil person produces evil things from the treasury of an evil heart. What you say flows from what is in your heart. **Luke 6:45**

Remember the goal is to win all financial battles!

Warriors Evaluation

Please circle the best answer that describes your warrior's heart.

1. *I have the potential to earn income.*
   a. *Totally Agree*
   b. *Partially Agree*
   c. *Disagree*

2. *I have unlimited access to money.*
   a. *Totally Agree*
   b. *Partially Agree*
   c. *Disagree*

3. *I eat one or more meals daily.*
   a. *Totally Agree*
   b. *Partially Agree*
   c. *Disagree*

4. *I have a place to sleep.*
   a. *Totally Agree*
   b. *Partially Agree*
   c. *Disagree*

5. *I am grateful for my job.*
   a. *Totally Agree*
   b. *Partially Agree*
   c. *Disagree*

6. *I pray for my boss daily.*
   a. *Totally Agree*
   b. *Partially Agree*
   c. *Disagree*

7. *I pray for my co-workers.*
   a. *Totally Agree*
   b. *Partially Agree*
   c. *Disagree*

8. *I am able to read and write.*
    a. *Totally Agree*
    b. *Partially Agree*
    c. *Disagree*

9. *I am able to see and hear.*
    a. *Totally Agree*
    b. *Partially Agree*
    c. *Disagree*

10. *I am able to walk and talk.*
    a. *Totally Agree*
    b. *Partially Agree*
    c. *Disagree*

11. *I have the potential to be employed.*
    a. *Totally Agree*
    b. *Partially Agree*
    c. *Disagree*

12. *I am capable of taking the metro/bus or walk/drive to work.*
    a. *Totally Agree*
    b. *Partially Agree*
    c. *Disagree*

13. *I have unlimited access to several job opportunities.*
    a. *Totally Agree*
    b. *Partially Agree*
    c. *Disagree*

14. *I have unlimited energy.*
    a. *Totally Agree*
    b. *Partially Agree*
    c. *Disagree*

15. *I have an abundance of confidence.*
    a. *Totally Agree*
    b. *Partially Agree*
    c. *Disagree*

16. *I am capable of writing down my financial goals.*
    a. *Totally Agree*
    b. *Partially Agree*
    c. *Disagree*

17. *I am capable of reading one financial book monthly.*
    a. *Totally Agree*
    b. *Partially Agree*
    c. *Disagree*

18. *I donate (tithe) ten percent of my income faithfully.*
    a. *Totally Agree*
    b. *Partially Agree*
    c. *Disagree*

19. *I save ten percent of my income faithfully.*
    a. *Totally Agree*
    b. *Partially Agree*
    c. *Disagree*

20. *I have the ability to establish multiple streams of savings.*
    a. *Totally Agree*
    b. *Partially Agree*
    c. *Disagree*

21. *I have the potential to start a business.*
    a. *Totally Agree*
    b. *Partially Agree*
    c. *Disagree*

22. *I have the ability to create multiple streams of income.*
    a. *Totally Agree*
    b. *Partially Agree*
    c. *Disagree*

23. *I choose wisely how money is used when it comes to me.*
    a. *Totally Agree*
    b. *Partially Agree*
    c. *Disagree*

24. *I limit the amount of money used to please my flesh.*
   a. *Totally Agree*
   b. *Partially Agree*
   c. *Disagree*

25. *I teach money how to work for me effectively.*
   a. *Totally Agree*
   b. *Partially Agree*
   c. *Disagree*

26. *I have the potential to be more generous.*
   a. *Totally Agree*
   b. *Partially Agree*
   c. *Disagree*

27. *I have the potential to save more money.*
   a. *Totally Agree*
   b. *Partially Agree*
   c. *Disagree*

28. *I have the ability to attract more money into my life.*
   a. *Totally Agree*
   b. *Partially Agree*
   c. *Disagree*

29. *I understand that there is no lack in God.*
   a. *Totally Agree*
   b. *Partially Agree*
   c. *Disagree*

30. *The Lord is my Shepherd therefore I shall not want.*
   a. *Totally Agree*
   b. *Partially Agree*
   c. *Disagree*

31. *God has given me the ability to create wealth.*
   a. *Totally Agree*
   b. *Partially Agree*
   c. *Disagree*

32. *I am blessed to be a blessing.*
    a. *Totally Agree*
    b. *Partially Agree*
    c. *Disagree*

33. *All my needs are met according to Christ Jesus.*
    a. *Totally Agree*
    b. *Partially Agree*
    c. *Disagree*

34. *I lack nothing.*
    a. *Totally Agree*
    b. *Partially Agree*
    c. *Disagree*

35. *I am wealthy.*
    a. *Totally Agree*
    b. *Partially Agree*
    c. *Disagree*

36. *I am financially responsible.*
    a. *Totally Agree*
    b. *Partially Agree*
    c. *Disagree*

37. *I am walking in my full inheritance from the Lord.*
    a. *Totally Agree*
    b. *Partially Agree*
    c. *Disagree*

38. *I have plenty of financial opportunities.*
    a. *Totally Agree*
    b. *Partially Agree*
    c. *Disagree*

39. *I have a short term (within twelve months) financial plan written down.*
    a. *Totally Agree*
    b. *Partially Agree*
    c. *Disagree*

40. *I have an intermediate (one to three years) financial plan written down.*
    a. *Totally Agree*
    b. *Partially Agree*
    c. *Disagree*

41. *I have a long term (three to five years) financial plan written down.*
    a. *Totally Agree*
    b. *Partially Agree*
    c. *Disagree*

42. *I believe that I am solely responsible for my current financial situation.*
    a. *Totally Agree*
    b. *Partially Agree*
    c. *Disagree*

43. *My savings account reflects my stewardship with money.*
    a. *Totally Agree*
    b. *Partially Agree*
    c. *Disagree*

44. *My investment account reflects my financial wisdom.*
    a. *Totally Agree*
    b. *Partially Agree*
    c. *Disagree*

45. *I have the potential of paying my bills on time.*
    a. *Totally Agree*
    b. *Partially Agree*
    c. *Disagree*

46. *I have the potential to save more and spend less.*
    a. *Totally Agree*
    b. *Partially Agree*
    c. *Disagree*

47. *I welcome financial wisdom from my peers.*
    a. *Totally Agree*
    b. *Partially Agree*
    c. *Disagree*

48. *I am successful at everything that I do.*
    a.   *Totally Agree*
    b.   *Partially Agree*
    c.   *Disagree*

49. *I have the potential to be financially independent.*
    a.   *Totally Agree*
    b.   *Partially Agree*
    c.   *Disagree*

50. *I have several opportunities to spend my time wisely.*
    a.   *Totally Agree*
    b.   *Partially Agree*
    c.   *Disagree*

51. *I am satisfied.*
    a.   *Totally Agree*
    b.   *Partially Agree*
    c.   *Disagree*

52. *I have the potential to use money to bless my mother and father.*
    a.   *Totally Agree*
    b.   *Partially Agree*
    c.   *Disagree*

53. *I thank God for daily financial increase.*
    a.   *Totally Agree*
    b.   *Partially Agree*
    c.   *Disagree*

54. *I am the beloved of the Lord.*
    a.   *Totally Agree*
    b.   *Partially Agree*
    c.   *Disagree*

55. *I am not fearful of poverty.*
    a.   *Totally Agree*
    b.   *Partially Agree*
    c.   *Disagree*

56. *I am a channel of abundance.*
    a. *Totally Agree*
    b. *Partially Agree*
    c. *Disagree*

57. *I am not anxious about money.*
    a. *Totally Agree*
    b. *Partially Agree*
    c. *Disagree*

58. *God is my all sufficiency.*
    a. *Totally Agree*
    b. *Partially Agree*
    c. *Disagree*

59. *The superabundance of Christ's riches belongs to me.*
    a. *Totally Agree*
    b. *Partially Agree*
    c. *Disagree*

60. *I am prospered in all my ways.*
    a. *Totally Agree*
    b. *Partially Agree*
    c. *Disagree*

Scores and Results:

*A score of 60 **a's** means you are ready for the frontline. Congratulations, grab a note-pad and pencil then proceed immediately to the next chapter.*

*Scores **less** than 60 **a's** means that you are not ready for the frontline so proceed to the next chapter with caution.*

*Scores of **b's** and **c's** means that you are not emotionally or spiritually equipped to fight by yourself. Ask a Holy Ghost Filled Fire Baptized child of God to mentor you before reading the next chapters.*

Chapter Two: Financial Prayer
Psalm 144: 1-2

Praise the Lord, who is my rock. He trains my hands to war and gives my fingers skill for battle. He is my loving ally and fortress, my tower of safety, my rescuer. He is my shield, and I take refuge in him. He makes the nations submit to me.

You don't need further instruction about baptisms, the laying on of hands, the resurrection of the dead, and eternal judgment. And so, God willing, we will move forward to further understanding.

Hebrews 6:2,3

Chapter Three

Basic Training
(Financial Boot Camp)

Chapter Three: Basic Financial Training

Basic training is the first step all entry level warriors must complete in order to win their financial battles. Entering the financial battlefield without basic training will always result in death.

If you have never gone through basic financial training, do not fear; this chapter will assist you in preparing properly for the most important war you will ever fight.

Don't be intimidated in any way by your enemies. This will be a sign to them that they are going to be destroyed, but that you are going to be saved, even by God himself.
Philippians 1:28

Basis Financial Training involves intense discipline and understanding so as to secure a strong foundation that produce victory after victory for generations. You are not a civilian citizen of this present world, so you must not get entangled with the affairs of this world.

You are a warrior for Christ; therefore you must become more concerned with the things of God, and identify the specific financial territory assigned to you for the taking.

Soldiers don't get tied up in the affairs of civilian life, for then they cannot please the officer who enlisted them. **2 Timothy 2:4**

The purpose of Basic Financial Training is to provide financial boot camp strategies and combat skills for entry level financial warriors. These strategies and tactics are to be used skillfully to fight your financial battles with more confidence. The information in this chapter provides detailed combat skills that will make your transition from entry level soldier to financial warrior mentality much easier.
<u>Completing basic financial training is crucial to achieving success.</u>

Wisdom has built her house; she has carved its seven columns. **Proverbs 9:1**

Basic Financial Training is an effective and strategic way to multiply your chances for financial success. Basic financial training is accomplished through acquiring financial combat skills that prepares you to use the seven principles of wisdom with power. You must spend time in preparation and training in order to win every battle. It is your responsibility as a warrior to secure your mind, body and soul with the proper financial intelligence information before entering the financial battlefield.

"You don't have enough faith," Jesus told them. "I tell you the truth, if you had faith even as small as a mustard seed, you could say to this mountain, 'Move from here to there,' and it would move. Nothing would be impossible." **Matthew 17:20**

Financial Combat Skill #1: Fear of the Lord

The Fear of the Lord provides many benefits. Wealth, perfect health and a long-life are promised to those who qualify.

Developing the Fear of the Lord eliminates the spirit of procrastination and the constant excuses for why you do not have enough money to help your pastor achieve the goal of spreading the gospel or helping family members who lack financial wisdom.

One of the facets of a financial warrior's faith is to be honest with God about their lack of financial wisdom. God can withstand anything. God want you to reach out to him daily for more insight and wisdom about your financial situations.

Fearing God is the beginning of wisdom. Try to face your doubts and fears about your financial situation forcefully and with confidence, knowing your reverence for God will release a successful economic plan that will bring prosperity into your home.

Individuals who fear God enjoy luxury and great success. Their homes are always filled with increased joy, peace and happiness, because the enemy cannot find a way to enter. God secures those who fear Him with warring angels.

Warring Angels are given specific instructions to protect the homes of all those who respect and honor God. Fearing God is the foundation for acquiring financial success without struggle and torment.

Do not fear poverty or lack. Fear only God! Who else can allow your heart to beat perfectly while you sleep? Who writes the beautiful songs for the birds to sing each day? Who makes the flowers bloom in the right season? Who sent his son Jesus to die on the cross for you?

If you allow God to enter your life, he will open up doors for you that were once closed. He will cause people to offer you opportunities that once were not available. Whatever you desire is in God, trust him and you will prosper.

God has no favorites. He loves all his Children. He rewards and judges us according to daily works. It is best to have a small amount of fear towards God, than to have great riches and no fear of God. Reach out for God's hand to guide your finances. Do not worry about how; just trust God to provide more financial wisdom each day that will teach you supernatural ways to break the chains of poverty off your life.

Fear of the Lord is the foundation of true wisdom. All who obey his commandments will grow in wisdom. **Psalm 111:10**

Fear of the Lord Financial Assessment
(Please Answer TRUE or FALSE)

1. I usually wait until I'm in trouble before reaching out to God.   _____

2. I do not send financial support to ministers who teach prosperity.   _____

3. I sometimes read the Bible on Sundays, maybe!   _____

4. I do not pray over my financial goals daily.   _____

5. I fear being poor.   _____

6. I do not pay my tithes.   _____

7. I am in constant fear about how to pay my bills.   _____

Total Number of TRUE Answers   _____

Total Number of FALSE Answers   _____

7 FALSE Answers equals ready for battle
6 or Less FALSE Answers equals Room for improvement
4 or more TRUE Answers equals (needs work ASAP)

<u>Ways to Apply Fear of the Lord Boot Camp Strategies to Your Finances</u>:

1. Fear God, by writing down all the financial goals God has already spoken into your spirit.

2. Create a one page plan for each financial goal.

3. Ask God for a financial mentor to guide you with your training.

4. Confess daily **"The Fear of the Lord is my strong foundation."**

5. Expect only victory when paying your bills on time.

6. Pay your tithes ahead of time.

7. Increase your seed sowing (giving to others) weekly.

Financial Combat Skill #2: Integrity

Integrity is having the characteristics of honesty and sincerity. Every financial goal must begin with integrity. You must develop a willing heart towards becoming financially independent. It is crucial that you understand the importance of integrity with daily financial increase.

Developing financial integrity means keeping your word and following through with all contracts, verbal or written. Understand that no one else is responsible for your financial failures. If God cannot trust you with $10; how can he trust you with millions?

Lack of financial integrity is one of the reasons why so many Christians are tormented by poverty and lack. You see, if you take a good look at your financial situation, you will see that God has always provided more than enough. But because many love the welfare system, all financial responsibilities are usually turned over to someone else. In addition, many turn their noses down on any message that educates them about becoming more responsible with their finances.

Being irresponsible with the income that God gives you and claiming that God wants you to be poor is a sign that you do not fear God. Integrity must be a priority with every dollar that God allows to enter your hands.

Spending your rent money at the beauty shop and then crying to your pastor for help will bring a curse on your family for generations to come. Be very careful how you try to manipulate God's ministers/teachers. God sees and knows all things, He can never be mocked! God distributes daily increase for all his children from heaven. Understand that you are reaping today exactly what you, your parents and grand parents sowed financially in the past. No more, no less!

A person who is fundamentally honest does not need a lesson about integrity. It will take integrity to save 10% of your income and to pay your bills on time. It takes integrity to follow through with financial goals and to seek counsel when feeling overwhelmed during your financial battles.

Integrity without financial wisdom produces poverty; and financial wisdom without integrity produce lack. Integrity is a powerful attribute that releases unlimited increase, abundance and overflow to all those who fear God. Integrity is glued to honesty, and acquiring this financial combat skill will bring great financial increase for you and your family for a life time.

The godly walk with integrity; blessed are their children who follow them.

Proverbs 20:7

Integrity Financial Assessment
(Please Answer TRUE or FALSE)

1. I balance my checkbook daily/weekly. _____
2. I am financially independent. _____
3. I have a written plan to pay each bill monthly. _____
4. I create a spending calendar/budget at the beginning of each month. _____
5. I have a plan to reduce spending. _____
6. I am debt free. _____
7. I pay my bills before due date. _____

Total Number of TRUE Answers _____
Total Number of FALSE Answers _____

7 TRUE Answers equals Ready for battle
6 or Less TRUE Answers equals Room for improvement
4 or more FALSE Answers equals (needs work ASAP)

Ways to Apply Integrity Boot Camp Strategies to Your Finances:

1. Practice being honest in paying your tithes.
2. Make good on all your promises.
3. Look at your financial situation as it is, not what you wish or desire.
4. Pay your taxes.
5. Declare war on impulse buying.
6. Read the book of Job (Bible) to learn more about a man with great integrity.
7. Be sincere with your feelings about money.

Financial Combat Skill #3: Discernment

Discernment is a combat skill allowing the Holy Spirit to display God's financial plans and ideas for your life. It is a process that increases the spiritual ability of God's children to perceive their financial plans scripturally. Discernment is an adventure in faith. It's more than just a skill.

The Holy Spirit works through scriptures to teach God's financial principles. Scripture shows God's priority for financial advancement. In order to discern God's financial plans for your life, you must get connected to scripture. It's the only way!

Individuals who do not spend time depositing the Word of God into their spirit are unable to experience the powerful skill of intelligent discernment. One of the roles of the Holy Spirit is to help us discern rightly. This is accomplished through the scriptures.

Some qualities of one who has a discerning spirit:
1. Believes the financial scriptures of God without doubt.
2. Loves to give.
3. Follows a life of integrity and righteousness with all financial increase.
4. Has two or more scriptural proof as examples that God wants them to increase financially.
5. Encourages others to read and apply financial scriptures for themselves.
6. Has compassion for those who lack intelligent discernment about prosperity.
7. Bold and confident with their savings plan.

Having intelligent discernment allows you to see what God sees. Intelligent discernment is having the eyes of God directly on your finances. Financial warriors must understand that the main reason for achieving financial freedom on planet earth is to become a funding resource for God. You are to position yourself to be a lender.

To develop intelligent discernment, you must have an ongoing daily relationship with The Lord Jesus Christ. Memorizing hundreds of financial scriptures without the ability to use them for advancement is not spiritual insight.

It is better to learn how to use one financial scripture effectively to get out of debt, rather than memorizing hundreds of scriptures with no power to change your financial situation.

God wants his children to be financial leaders to the nation. You were created for this battle because God knew that he could trust you to establish financial dominion in the earth. You are more than equipped to fight and win this war because you have Christ on your side!

Let those who are wise understand these things. Let those with discernment listen carefully. The paths of the Lord are true and right, and righteous people live by walking in them. But in those paths sinners stumble and fall. **Hosea 14:9**

Discernment Financial Assessment
(Please Answer TRUE or FALSE)

1. I get excited about my financial assignments from God.   _____

2. I am currently enrolled in a bible study group that focuses on finance. _____

3. I have a copy of the book "Daily Financial Journal."   _____

4. I plead the "Blood of Jesus" over my finances daily.   _____

5. I can hear the Holy Spirit daily assignments for my finances.   _____

6. I listen to the **Word** one or more hours daily.   _____

7. I keep a discernment journal
   (Writings about your time spent with God).   _____

Total Number of TRUE Answers   _____

Total Number of FALSE Answers   _____

7 TRUE Answers equals ready for battle
6 or Less TRUE Answers equals Room for improvement
4 or more FALSE Answers equals (needs work ASAP)

Ways to Apply Discernment Boot Camp Strategies to Your Finances:

1. Listen to the New Testament Weekly.

2. Read the Entire Bible Every Quarter.

3. Enroll in a Bible Study Course for Financial Improvement.

4. Fast during the First Seven Days of Each Month.

5. Practice Daily Communion (Plead the Blood of Jesus on your finances).

6. Write in a Discernment Journal Daily.

7. Train your ears gate to listen in the Spirit for Daily Assignments.

Financial Combat Skill #4: Knowledge

Knowledge is the awareness and understanding of the facts, truths or information gained in the form of experience or learning. In other words, knowledge is what the brain knows. Knowledge is not wisdom. Knowledge is one of the doorways to wisdom.

The more financial knowledge you seek, the closer you get at achieving your goals. However, this does not mean you are financially wise. You become financially wise only when all **Seven Basic Finance Combat Skills** are working together at the same time.

Financial knowledge is of no value unless you are able to put it into practice. Acquired financial knowledge must turn into action. Action must be applied to every sermon you hear and every book that you read. Otherwise, you've wasted precious time.

Acquiring a lot of information about prosperity, wealth and riches is necessary for growth. However, information becomes knowledge only if you can use it to change or improve your life.

Financial knowledge is the gateway to increase wealth and riches. Make it a daily priority. Eliminate fear of poverty and increase your ability to succeed. Open your ears to knowledge on how to fight and win your financial war with great power and boldness.

Beware of those who possess financial information but are powerless. It is impossible for someone to know about God's financial principles, yet unable to use it for themselves. This includes pastors who preach against prosperity.

Those offended by others prospering are usually in a state of lack and fears poverty. They are unable to use financial scriptures to discern God's economic plans. You will never find a person with wealth and riches speaking against prosperity.

In addition, be very gentle and show compassion to ministers who simply do not have knowledge about God's financial wisdom. Continue to pray for those who see in part, and ask God for mercy on their soul. You must have compassion for your brothers and sisters who lack financial knowledge and wisdom. God will bless you for being kind.

In view of all this, make every effort to respond to God's promises. Supplement your faith with a generous provision of moral excellence, and moral excellence with knowledge, and knowledge with self-control, and self-control with patient endurance, and patient endurance with godliness, and godliness with brotherly affection, and brotherly affection with love for everyone. **2 Peter 1:5-7**

Financial Knowledge Assessment
(Please Answer TRUE or FALSE)

1. I invest one hour daily in financial education. _____
2. I read 12 or more financial books annually. _____
3. My income potential increases yearly. _____
4. I have a savings account established for every financial goal. _____
5. I pray for those who speak against my ability to increase financially. _____
6. I look for ways to bless my financial mentors. _____
7. I always feel confident about my financial decisions. _____

Total Number of TRUE Answers _____

Total Number of FALSE Answers _____

7 TRUE Answers ready for battle
6 or Less TRUE Answers equals Room for improvement
4 or more FALSE Answers equals (needs work ASAP)

Ways to Apply Knowledge Boot Camp Strategies to Your Finances:

1. Develop a habit of spending one hour or more seeking financial knowledge daily.
2. Use your knowledge about finance to make wise financial decisions.
3. Discipline yourself to create multiple streams of savings.
4. Dominate your mind with ways to acquire financial stability.
5. Behave like one who has an abundance of financial wisdom.
6. Access financial power through reading books that stimulate your mind.
7. Increase your financial success by developing one new positive financial habit every month.

Financial Combat Skill #5: Understanding

Understanding is the ability to think and act flexibly with what you know. This would be a great time to develop a three-dimensional thinking strategy: the ability to think, see and hear in both the physical and spiritual realms.

Learning the facts about financial increase, overflow and management can be very overwhelming, but learning all these facts is not the same as understanding.

Many individuals have read countless books, attended seminars, even achieved degrees in finance; however, most of these individuals are not able to apply the knowledge of what they've learned to get themselves out of debt.

Understanding requires involvement. It means physically getting involved by applying the knowledge received about your credit report and effectively making changes for financial advancement.

The inability to get involved is a sign that an invisible vale has been placed over your eyes. This is the reason why some people can do the same things, but one will cultivate success, while the other produces failure. This invisible vale keeps away false believers from acquiring peace with God's inheritance.

Only God's children can acquire the inheritance from the Lord with peace. Unfaithfulness and doubt cannot access understanding. To remove this invisible vale, and receive the gift of understanding, you must accept Jesus Christ as Lord and Savior. There is no other way!

To those who listen to my teaching, more understanding will be given, and they will have an abundance of knowledge. But for those who are not listening, even what little understanding they have will be taken away from them. **Matthew 13:12**

There are different levels of hearing; therefore we have different levels of understanding. Those with limited amount of financial knowledge can only understand at a limited level. While individuals who invest time daily to increase their financial knowledge will understand much more and achieve greater success.

Individuals who understand their own financial situation usually develop the ability to teach others. Teaching others how to improve their financial situation is a great attribute of one who has received the gift of understanding from God. This precious gift must be cherished and used for increasing personal value for greater good. Those who cherish financial understanding will always prosper.

Above all, you must realize that no prophecy in Scripture ever came from the prophet's own understanding, or from human initiative. No, those prophets were moved by the Holy Spirit, and they spoke from God. **2 Peter 1:20,21**

Understanding Financial Assessment
(Please Answer TRUE or FALSE)

1. I apply action to my financial education plan. _____

2. I review my financial goals daily. _____

3. I share my financial knowledge with others. _____

4. I review my credit report annually. _____

5. I am a master of my money. _____

6. I listen attentively to what God says about finance. _____

7. I have one or more financial mentors. _____

Total Number of TRUE Answers _____

Total Number of FALSE Answers _____

7 TRUE Answers equals ready for battle
6 or Less TRUE Answers equals Room for improvement
4 or more FALSE Answers equals (needs work ASAP)

Ways to Apply Understanding Boot Camp Strategies to Your Finances:

1. Seek God early in the morning regarding daily financial plans.

2. Put together an action plan for every financial goal.

3. Invest quality time with financial goals.

4. Trust God with all financial goals.

5. Write out 100 simple things you could do to win each financial battle.

6. Draw a picture declaring victory with your financial warfare.

7. Develop a financial plan in three dimensions.

Financial Combat Skill #6: Good Judgment

Good judgment involves having all the facts and handling them with fairness. Your current financial situation is a clear reflection of past decisions. When one decides not to work or to purchase items on credit that they cannot afford, this is an example of bad judgment. When you decide to pay your tithes and help those who lack financial wisdom, this is an example of good judgment.

Everyday is ordained as the best day of the year, so embrace life with more passion. Your daily financial decisions are steps towards preparing your financial future. Be vigilant when it comes to spending without a plan. Financial decisions made today about savings or spending will meet up with you in the future.

There are many today who wish they had started a savings account before graduating elementary school. There are many reading this book right now, who wished they had this information years ago. The bottom line is that your ability to make good financial decisions happens daily. Every second of the day you are given another chance to change your financial future. Be smart and choose to make good judgment which increases your chances of winning your financial battles successfully.

You may not have the house or job that you want today. You may not even like your boss and coworkers, but you can decide today to make better decisions with your finances. The possibilities are numerous once you decide to use financial knowledge skillfully throughout each day.

Financial freedom is the result of making good judgment with daily income. Financial bondage is making financial decisions without a plan. God is a planner; therefore his children must learn about effective planning strategies that positions them for financial leadership.

A great act of faith is when an individual decides to increase his/her financial wisdom and uses it to please God. God's economic plan prepares his children to make good financial judgments. That's why God's financial planning will work for those who consider themselves poor as well as those with thoughts of wealth. God's economic plan will work for anyone who chooses to use it, bond or free.

Making good financial judgments must be the first step you make each day. Learn to use good judgment when using credit cards and equity in your home. Seek out financial wisdom first before making hasty decisions. Develop a written plan to pay your bills before they are due. You are as powerful and strong as your ability to make good financial decisions. God's economic plan is all you will ever need!

I, Wisdom, live together with good judgment.
I know where to discover knowledge and discernment.
Proverbs 8:12

Good Judgment Financial Assessment
(Please Answer TRUE or FALSE)

1. My bills are organized and categorized. _____
2. I pay my tithes first. _____
3. My credit score is in excellent condition. _____
4. I have an emergency fund with at least one month's household budget. _____
5. I contribute to a retirement fund monthly. _____
6. My net worth increases annually. _____
7. I put aside weekly savings for annual family vacation. _____

Total Number of TRUE Answers _____

Total Number of FALSE Answers _____

7 TRUE Answers equals ready for battle
6 or Less TRUE Answers equals Room for improvement
4 or more FALSE Answers equals (needs work ASAP)

Ways to Apply Good Judgment Boot Camp Strategies to Your Finances:

1. Put aside 10% of all your income for investing in your "Victory Fund".
2. Know that you have the ability to make excellent financial decisions.
3. Meet with a financial planner.
4. Set up a savings account for your ten year goals.
5. Create a "Declaration of War" one-page financial strategy for every bill.
6. Maximize your financial strength by reviewing your one year, five year, ten year, and lifetime plans with your financial mentor.
7. Declare financial independence for your household.

Financial Combat Skill #7: Common Sense and Success

Common sense and success is essential for financial success. Common sense and success requires daily discipline. Steadily taking action with your financial goals will always produce success. Achieving common sense and success is progressive. It increases each time you apply action.

There are no short cuts or days off in this financial war. Our enemies **NEVER** take a day off. Therefore you must stay focused, and develop habits that command you to follow through with the financial goal of being financially independent.

Developing a common sense and success mentality are results of becoming more valuable to your family, friends, and the community. Financial warriors must apply 100% effort daily in order to be productive for the body of Christ.

Do not undervalue who you are. You are a conqueror through Christ. You were meant to live in luxury and abundance. Five of us can chase one hundred of our enemies and one hundred of us can chase ten thousand. God will always make sure that you prosper if you obey his Word. Success is inevitable with God on your side.

If there is doubt of any kind that you are unable to achieve financial independence, it will be impossible for you to stay focused on victory. Be gentle with yourself and ask God for increased faith. None of God's children started at the top. God's children are being trained constantly to live effectively in the spirit, and less in the flesh.

In order to achieve continuous common sense and success you must climb one ladder at a time. Learn to take small steps towards victory. This kind of financial power will not come overnight. Common sense and success is an honor for those who complete basic financial boot camp using God's economic plan.

Achieving all seven financial combat skills means that you are packing power to speak to things as if they were. Making it this far means that you are no longer afraid to take a good look at your financial situation. It means you are ready to face your enemies who once had a hose hooked up to your savings account.

Completing basic financial boot camp means you have entered a level of financial confidence knowing that God fights for all his children **until** they win.

Remember the Lord your God. He is the one who gives you the power to be successful, in order to fulfill the covenant he confirmed to your ancestors with an oath.
Deuteronomy 8:18

Common Sense and Success Financial Assessment
(Please Answer TRUE or FALSE)

1. I stay focused on my financial goals.   _____
2. I do not procrastinate with my bills.   _____
3. My family and friends can count on me financially.   _____
4. I look for ways to support my community financially.   _____
5. I meet with a financial mentor monthly.   _____
6. I bring my daily financial plans to God for review.   _____
7. I pray for financial increase for my boss and clients.   _____

Total Number of TRUE Answers   _____
Total Number of FALSE Answers   _____

7 TRUE Answers equals ready for battle
6 or Less TRUE Answers equals Room for improvement
4 or more FALSE Answers equals (needs work ASAP)

Ways to Apply Common Sense and Successful Boot Camp Strategies to Your Finances:

1. Develop the discipline of following through on all financial goals.
2. Stay focused on your plans for getting out of debt.
3. Repeat this quote daily **"All My Needs Are Met Today Through Christ."**
4. Prepare a giving plan for the needs in your family and community.
5. Carve out a special time of day to bring written financial plans to God in prayer.
6. Apply 100% effort towards your savings/investment plans.
7. Take some form of action everyday.

Chapter Three Review: Financial Boot Camp

Fear of God:
Obey God's laws and commands in order to experience financial success.

Integrity:
Be honest in all financial transactions. Review your credit report annually and make changes for advancement.

Discernment:
Seek God for insight regarding his vision for your financial success.
Develop this skill and learn to see what God sees for your financial future.

Knowledge:
Read books about financial management and strategies. Apply immediate action to every sermon, book and seminar that teaches how to become financially independent.

Understanding:
Share financial knowledge with family members and friends.
Increase your understanding about finance by teaching others the same principles that worked for you after you have applied it for yourself.

Good Judgment:
Make wise decisions in spending, savings and investments. Create a "Declaration of War" for every bill.

Common Sense & Success:
Follow through on giving 100% effort toward all financial goals.
Practice diligence and never give up. No more shadowboxing! Fight to win every time!

Chapter Three: Voice Activated Financial Confessions

It is written: I am the head and not the tail.

It is written: I am blessed coming in; and blessed going out.

It is written: The fear of the Lord is my foundation of true knowledge.

It is written: Integrity and honesty always protects me.

It is written: My children will be blessed, when I walk with integrity.

It is written: Insight is a beloved family member of mine.

It is written: Discernment allows me to see how God sees.

It is written: Common Sense and Success belong to me.

It is written: The Greater One is in me.

It is written: I can do all things through Christ.

It is written: God has given me divine wisdom, direction and understanding.

It is written: I am the body of Christ.

It is written: God who has given me the power to get wealth.

It is written: No weapons formed against me shall prosper.

It is written: Wisdom is better when I have money.

It is written: Kind words are like honey.

It is written: Those who listen to instructions will prosper.

It is written: Better to have little, with godliness, than to be rich and dishonest.

Chapter Three Financial Prayer
Luke 2: 68-79

Praise the Lord, the God of Israel,
    because he has visited and redeemed his people.
He has sent us a mighty Savior
    from the royal line of his servant David,
just as he promised
    through his holy prophets long ago.
Now we will be saved from our enemies
    and from all who hate us.
He has been merciful to our ancestors
    by remembering his sacred covenant—
the covenant he swore with an oath
    to our ancestor Abraham.
We have been rescued from our enemies
    so we can serve God without fear,
In holiness and righteousness
    for as long as we live.

And you, my little son,
    will be called the prophet of the Most High,
    because you will prepare the way for the Lord.
You will tell his people how to find salvation
    through forgiveness of their sins.
Because of God's tender mercy,
    the morning light from heaven is about to break upon us,
to give light to those who sit in darkness and in the shadow of death,
    And to guide us to the path of peace."

For we are not fighting against flesh and blood enemies, but against evil rulers and authorities of the unseen world, against mighty powers in this dark world, and against evil spirits in the heavenly places.

Ephesians 6:12

Chapter Four

The Attack Part I
(Dirty Financial Secrets Exposed)

Chapter Four: The Attack (Dirty Financial Secrets Exposed)

Financial adversity comes to all people. Hence, you are responsible for choices and behaviors regarding monies that flow directly through your hands each day. Rich or poor, black or white, Christian or non-Christian; financial strongholds are global threats with global effects which consequently can affect every aspect of your life. Financial strongholds are pickpockets who are always hungry for victims, so open your spiritual and physical eyes. NOW!

The dirty financial secrets of financial strongholds are exposed so that you may learn to become diligent and do whatever it takes to be more responsible with daily financial increase. This chapter will encourage you to seek intelligent discernment for direction on how to use God's money properly, not to become an easy prey to financial strongholds.

A financial stronghold's motto is to find a need that caters to the flesh and fill it. Individuals who become a financial stronghold to others have many faces and are connected to a very lucrative business. Financial strongholds usually dominate a particular product or service. They often introduce themselves as a solution to a problem. Financial strongholds are usually business men and women who want to make money solely by using the lust of the flesh as their main campaign for recruiting consumers.

The following are usually seen as easy prey to those who are motivated in the business of becoming a financial stronghold to others.

- Liars
- Compulsive Gamblers
- Alcoholics
- Those Who Lack Financial Knowledge
- Workaholics
- The Uneducated
- Drug Addicts
- Sex Addicts
- Those Who Envy Others

Anyone who desperately desires more money than they have is the perfect target for a financial stronghold. Financial strongholds make big profits from people who live to please their flesh and not the spirit of the Lord. For as long as you have a need to satisfy your fleshly desires, there will always be a financial stronghold to provide a service or product for a fee.

Keeping someone in financial bondage is a major source of income for the families of those who provide products and services to those motivated by the desires of their flesh.

Financial strongholds stay in business and make money by satisfying the desires of those they prey upon. Financial strongholds thrive on consumers who need or want more than they can afford to have. These consumers can be easily manipulated through advertisements that display the pickpocket's products and services as "affordable" and "necessary."

There are laws regulating the financial stronghold industry, but they rarely benefit the consumer. It is appalling to see the number of requests that come in the mail enticing consumers to apply for another credit card, even though the consumer is already unable to pay off a current one. It is even more shocking to see what a check cashing establishment will do to those in need of a "payday loan."

Second mortgages are another form of financial bondage waiting for those who desire to have more before they can afford it. Many families have lost their homes to foreclosures and bankruptcies because they were not prepared financially to take on the first mortgage much less the second. Keep a keen eye on your money before a financial stronghold steals it from you.

Pickpocket Marketing Tactics to Stay Away From:
- Bad Credit, No Credit, No Problem!
- Rent to Own
- Buy Now, Pay Later
- No Money Down
- Payday Loans
- Secured and Unsecured Loans
- Warranty
- No Credit Check
- Second Mortgage
- Just Try It!
- No Collateral Needed
- High Pressure Sales
- Discounts with Another Purchase
- Going Out of Business Sale
- Everyone's Pre-Approved

There are fifteen financial strongholds the enemy uses as weapons to steal your savings, property and investments. These strongholds are carefully disguised and renamed as distractions to keep God's children from inheriting the blessings of the Lord. A lack of financial wisdom often produce debt and out of control spending. It's no secret: those who lack money and financial wisdom suffer greatly.

Wisdom is even better when you have money. Both are a benefit as you go through life.
Ecclesiastes 7:11

Chapter Pre-View—(Financial Codes)

The inability to advance financially often stems from ideas or suggestions that a financial stronghold uses over and over to attach itself to your financial increase. Financial strongholds have **three goals** in mind for all their victims: to steal, kill and destroy. Take your time as you try to understand what code is attached to your current financial situation and what strategies are needed to be implemented in order to break the yoke of financial strongholds off your wallet.

Code Green (Internal Financial Disasters)
#1 Selfish Ambition
#2 Dissension
#3 Division

Code Orange (Financial Viruses)
#4 Quarreling
#5 Hostility
#6 Outburst of Anger

Code Yellow (Financial Threat)
#7 Jealousy
#8 Envy

Code White (Financial Emergency)
#9 Idolatry
#10 Sorcery

Code Green

Internal Financial Disasters

Financial Stronghold #1: Selfish Ambition

Selfish Ambition is the first financial stronghold used as a weapon to keep God's children in financial bondage. Selfish ambition is an internal financial disaster that supports the lust of the flesh and is designed to steal your self-worth.

Selfish ambition means self-centered and self-serving. Low self-esteem is a major cause of selfishness. Set backs and leftovers are very friendly with those who are selfish. Every selfish person is a potential enemy; stay away! At the root of every problem lies someone with a selfish ambition.

Being selfish is a popular way where many poison themselves from the inside out. The soul is already decaying; therefore selfishness attaches itself to the individual and takes root just like a cancerous cell and spreads all throughout their finances. The financial attack of selfish ambition is highly effective against those who do not like to share.

Selfish ambition is an act of having one end in view: oneself. The word financial plan gives selfish people a headache. "Tracking income and expenses" is a dirty phrase for individuals who practice selfishness. No accountability is necessary.

It is impossible for individuals with selfish ambitions to give. Rampant materialism appears to be the middle names for those with selfish ambition. Many of these individuals eliminate prosperity from their lives simply because they are unable to give to family, friends or the church.

In order to fight the spirit of selfish ambition effectively you must become a champion at giving freely to others from the heart.

Selfishness is a stronghold that blocks financial increase. Refusing to write down financial goals is an example of an individual who is being attacked from within. The demonic stronghold of selfishness loves stealing financial goals and dreams. Lack of financial goals makes it easier to spend irresponsibly. This very act pleases Satan.

The words "Mine, Mine" are constantly on the minds of those possessed by the spirit of selfishness. Selfish Ambition candidates do not seek out financial advisors or mentors. They seek out those who mirror their behavior. However, fighting the spirit of selfish ambition will take power and strength. Seek financial advice from a financial mentor, and write down your financial goals. Prepare yourself for victory.

Those who practice selfishness are more likely to be corrupted by the company they keep. Selfishness has no sense of time. Selfish people usually show up late for work or waste other people's time by being late for appointments.

Lack of time management is costly. Wasting hours complaining to your friends about your inability to pay your bills is a clear sign that you are selfish and choosing to allow an internal financial disaster to run its course. Being selfish delays blessings.

*Then Jesus said to his disciples, "If any of you want to be my follower, you must turn from your selfish ways, take up your cross, and follow me. **Matthew 16:24***

Selfish individuals usually spend more than what they earn. Those affected by selfish ambitions make perfect consumers for financial strongholds. Basic financial tips are ignored. Their favorite words are "Give it to me" and "I want it now."

Selfish people often suffer greatly due to lack of vision. Fighting this financial stronghold faithfully means learning to be content in all things and working at creating a clear financial vision that involves helping others.

Examples of how to win the financial battle of selfish ambition:

1. Register and attend a Joyce Meyers conference to learn simple and effective ways to overcome the spirit of selfishness. Joyce Meyers is a powerful sister in Christ who is not afraid to share her personal struggles and triumphs in order to empower those who are serious about serving the Lord. You can learn more about Joyce Myers Ministries by visiting www. jm.org.

2. Read about the results of Absalom's selfish ambitions in 2 Samuel (The Bible). Learn about the cost of selfishness. Take a good look at your life and create a list of friends that reflect your selfish ways. Ask God for forgiveness and begin by taking small steps to change your selfish ways so as to attract friends who are generous, kind, loyal and prosperous.

3. Volunteer thirty minutes or more monthly helping to improve the financial situation of family members, friends or neighbors. Share stories how you have increased your savings simply by eliminating the spirit of selfishness from your life.

4. Break the cycle of poverty and pay your bills one month ahead. Begin by establishing a special savings account with the eventual goal of paying basic utility bills one month ahead.

5. Treat all your co-workers to lunch; this is a great seed to sow to remove the spirit of selfishness on the job.

6. Donate one week of your salary to purchase supplies for a local school. This act of kindness will increase your finances abundantly.

7. Sell everything you own and sign up for missionary work. Use a portion of the money responsibly to establish a financial portfolio with savings and investments that will produce financial increase long term. Use another portion of the money to teach missionaries how to set up a financial portfolio for themselves.

Financial Stronghold #2: Dissension

Dissension is an internal financial disaster used as a weapon to keep children of God in financial distress. Dissension supports the lust of the flesh and is an internal financial disaster that usually destroys partnerships.

Dissension is another battle that germinates from the inside and works its way to the outside. Dissension is a battle of disagreements or a difference of opinion. Individuals who welcome this financial stronghold into their lives usually have a strong belief in lack and poverty.

Dissension steals time (**money**) by arguing over and over about the same thing. Dissension distributors are not looking for a solution. Intense inner pain forces dissension lovers to waste time and money arguing instead of coming into agreement for a greater good.

Dissension carriers often tell lies that start fights and breaks partnerships that could have brought in millions of dollars to build schools, hospitals and provide quality health care for God's children. The spirit of dissension is an effective financial attack against God's children because it uses a weapon that kills all partnerships.

The spirit of dissension often follows those with a competitive drive. Competition occurs when someone believes that there is limited resource. Thoughts of limitation always produce cravings that increase lack. However, there is no need for competition. You are capable of creating your own wealth, prosperity and success.

There is an abundance of opportunities for everyone. There is no limit to the production of ideas that can produce billions. God is the infinite, unlimited, omnipresent, owner of all things in heaven and earth. Refuse to believe the lie that the only way to have success is to compete with others. God's children do not compete, they create. God's children are known for creating successful partnerships that bring him glory.

The spirit of dissension also forces many to disagree with ideas of reduce spending. There is no cooperation when an individual have made up their mind to become disagreeable. However, in order to live a life filled with prosperity and increase, you must partner and agree to support other's ability to succeed. To fight the spirit of dissension boldly; come in agreement with those who can teach you how to become financially responsible.

Recognize that the spirit of dissension is an invisible financial war being used as a distraction to remove you from your post. This is the time for you to understand the role of conflict.

It is not important who does the planting, or who does the watering. What's important is that God makes the seed grow. **1 Corinthians 3:7**

Conflict is a great friend of dissension. A conflict usually occurs when a mental struggle is present resulting from internal and external needs not being met. This mental struggle is designed to weaken your desires of becoming financially independent, and if not managed effectively will push all good intended for your life into the lives of others who manage conflict patiently.

Successful Conflict Resolution Strategies:
- Learn to negotiate every financial transaction
- Always be the first to apologize
- Focus on a win-win outcome
- Encourage others to share their ideas
- Listen more, talk less

Examples of how to win the financial battle of dissension:
1. Work hard at finding a common ground to agree with others. This simple act will eliminate dissension of all kinds.
2. Stop blaming others for your unhappiness. Take responsibility for your thinking. Realize the unlimited resources that surround you.
3. Acknowledge the importance of others by asking for their opinions.
4. Embrace your financial mission by helping others to create their own success.
5. Teach a class on "How to Master Dissension from the Inside Out."
6. Create partnerships that multiply your savings for three or more generations.
7. Remind yourself that you have the capability to create million dollar ideas that produce more than enough wealth to provide secure jobs for families globally.

Financial Stronghold #3: Division

Division is an internal financial disaster used as a weapon to keep God's children in financial anxiety. A divided mind can cause great danger. The spirit of division is a firm supporter of the lust of the flesh and is an internal financial disaster that pushes away the goodness of God.

The spirit of division occurs when you think in error. The belief of someone who thinks in error is usually in contrast to God. Thinking in error often rejects the advice of others and perceives their own views to be the only true facts. Many false prophets, teachers, believers, and pastors possess this trait.

Division is created through your own imagination. Statements such as, "God does not want me to prosper", or "It is God's will for me to be poor" are both false statements. The financial stronghold of division is effective only if you allow errors in your thinking to replace the Word of God.

You cannot embrace the spirit of division and enjoy the goodness of the Lord. Your blessings often are delivered through the hands of someone you cannot get along with. The person you cannot get along with at this time has your next opportunity for increase. He or she is sent with an assignment to bless you. Stay focused on preparing yourself to receive instead of finding fault with the people God sends to bless you with opportunities for wealth and riches.

It is your job as a child of God to live in harmony with everyone. God chose you to bring light to your job, your home, your friends and your enemies. Division should never be allowed to enter your thoughts. You were sent with the love of God to encourage unity and agreement between all people. You must get along with your neighbors and treat others the same way you would like to be treated.

The spirit of division has cost the body of Christ more money than all infidelity put together. Money that could be used to establish free child care nationwide is sent elsewhere due to the inability to get along with each other.

Do not feel discouraged if you are constantly in a verbal battle everywhere you go. This is a sign that God is desperately trying to get a blessing to you. If you are currently being attacked by division, break free now. Make a choice to get under an anointed leadership that teaches the truth about Jesus Christ, creator of all things great and small.

This is not the time to turn your back on God. Release all desire of controlling God's plans to experience success through you. Release all financial struggles and goals to the Almighty. Fight this financial stronghold effectively by eliminating all thinking that limits God's greatness in you.

I appeal to you, dear brothers and sisters, by the authority of our Lord Jesus Christ, to live in harmony with each other. Let there be no divisions in the church. Rather, be of one mind, united in thought and purpose. **1 Corinthians 1:10**

<u>Examples of how to win the financial battle of division:</u>
1. Build alliances with family and friends by supporting their plans and ideas for financial growth.
2. Become more interested in helping others succeed by recommending a book or a mentor who could bring more clarity to their financial plans.
3. Study the Word of God for yourself so that you will not lose any more blessings.
4. Never get distracted from your goal of being a mighty financial warrior; you are needed immediately to advance to the frontline to secure more wealth for the Body of Christ.
5. Watch out for false teachers who try to steal your inheritance with words of trickery.
6. Stay away from people who fight against God's Word. They do not stand a chance against Yahweh!
7. Ask God for a copy of his economic plan for your life and use it to express love towards everyone.

<u>Internal Financial Disaster Summary-Code Green</u>

Internal Attack #1
Selfish Ambition: It is impossible for individuals with selfish ambitions to give. This internal financial attack pushes away success and prosperity. This battle cannot be fought by celebrating self-destructive behaviors. Fight this financial internal attack by becoming more generous.

Internal Attack #2
Dissension: Fighting this internal financial attack takes strength. Agreeing to establish a savings and investment account is one way to kill this enemy. When things change, whether it's a job loss, divorce or business failure, accept the new reality and make financial adjustments quickly. Avoid a long term financial battle and agree to be responsible.

Internal Attack #3
Division: Disagreeing with others is thinking in error. This internal attack seeks to control people and sees the opposite of reality. Fight this enemy by re-reading this book until all thinking line up with God's economic will for your life.

Code Orange

Financial Viruses

Financial Stronghold #4: Quarreling

Quarreling is a financial virus used as a weapon to keep God's children in chaos. Quarreling is known for its strong commitment to the lust of the flesh and is a financial virus that often steals the tithes and makes many lawyers very rich.

The goal of a financial virus is to completely strip you of all future savings and investments. Quarreling is an effective attack used against many because it accomplishes its goal every time.

Just take a trip on your next day off to a divorce court in your city. Better yet, look at the financial state of your family and your friends who go through a divorce. Quarreling is at the root of every divorce; it must be prevented in order to win this financial war.

Unhappy people love to quarrel. Many of these individuals make it their goal to pick an argument or a fight as part of their daily ritual. Individuals who suffer from internal pain often try to "medicate" themselves by releasing a quarreling virus onto other people.

Individuals who love to quarrel are usually in so much pain that the only solution for them to feel better is to reproduce that same feeling in others. Thus, a financial virus is released through quarreling, to reproduce itself.

Let's prevent this financial virus from spreading by going back to the beginning of this chapter. Work on selfish ambitions, dissension and division. God's children are only at this level of attack because they refused to heed the code green warning signs. God gave these warnings thousands of years ago. Many will not be permitted to inherit the Kingdom of God if they continue to live this way. Read Galatians Chapter 5 in the Bible to learn more.

During my research, I came across startling information regarding the body of Christ and Divorce. Christians' divorce rate is just as high as non-Christians'. Divorce lawyers are planning vacations ahead of time because they know the demand for their services will be very high for Christians infected with this deadly financial virus.

Lawyers can increase their future savings as they wait patiently for the children of God to make copies of a behavior that clearly glorifies the flesh. The money that the divorce industry produces is mind boggling. Can you not see the insanity?

Quarreling is an effective financial virus because many are sometimes clueless about its ability to copy and replicate. You can prevent this financial virus from entering your home simply by learning the principles of how to get along with your family, your friends, and your neighbors.

Some financial viruses re-write themselves completely each time. No one quarrels by themselves. It takes one person to infect the other, thereby copying the virus without the knowledge of the individual.

Do you not see the attacks on your family? Many are so separated from God that they are unable to see the enemy coming. Wake up! Snap out of financial denial, and take control.

Families are creating first, second and third generation children who infect each other with the financial virus of quarreling. Quarreling over and over again about the same thing means a demonic force is working against the family. This is not the Will of God for his children. Kill this financial virus by getting control over demonic thoughts and behaviors that can cause great harm to your family, your friends and your community.

Individuals who are carriers of the financial virus of quarreling are responsible for every court battle. Every lawsuit stems from a carrier of this financial virus. False insurance claims, child custody and spousal support battles are also results from the financial virus of quarreling. Imagine how much money is being used to fund the desires of our flesh.

Quarreling always leaves visible signs and is very harmful. Quarreling is often experienced by those who live to please the flesh and is a major attack on the Body of Christ. It must be stopped before you become a carrier yourself. Learn to forgive those who speak negatively about you. Learn to walk away and save your money.

Then Peter came to him and asked, "Lord, how often should I forgive someone who sins against me? Seven Times?" "No, not seven times," Jesus replied, "but seventy times seven!" **Matthew 18:21,22**

Examples of how to win the battle of quarreling:
1. Keep your peace when someone offends you. Learn to keep your mouth shut.
2. Learn effective communication skills that put the needs of others before your own.
3. Listen more, talk less and receive more.
4. Take every financial problem to God, giving thanks for the answer.
5. Wake up singing joyful songs, welcoming God's unlimited increase.
6. Bless your enemies at all times and you will be blessed more abundantly.
7. Get rid of the snakes (friends) who speak death about your spouse and children.

Financial Stronghold #5: Hostility

Hostility is a financial virus used as a weapon to keep many trapped in debt. Hostility loves to give a hand to the lust of the flesh and is a financial virus that produces lack.

Hostility is a form of anger that willfully refuses to accept evidence about their financial situation. This financial virus blinds the carrier; therefore, he/she cannot detect the truth being deleted from their awareness about overspending. An excellent example is an individual who refuses to work, yet continues to spend and borrow.

The spirit of hostility does not reconsider. Individuals who suppress the truth about their finances make great consumers. Be proactive and look for ways to improve your financial situation. Refusing to meet with a financial advisor or mentor is a clear sign that this virus has taken up residence in your home.

<u>Attributes of one who is a carrier of the financial virus of hostility may include:</u>
1. Ready to fight or argue about rising cost of inflation.
2. Sarcastic about their financial situation.
3. Disinterested about family or friends financial issues.
4. Inability to forgive or forget those who borrowed money and are unable to make payments.
5. A desire to protect oneself at any price.
6. Vulnerable to constant bank fees.
7. Displaying defensive and paranoid reactions when asked questions about their savings and investments.
8. Craving sympathy when he/she experiences a job loss.
9. Refusing to participate in any form of financial growth activities.
10. Unclear about financial goals and plays the role of a victim.

Having one or more credit-cards maxed out is a clear sign you are in serious financial trouble. However, a carrier of the financial virus hostility will deny this fact and continue to shop, just to prove a point that supports their misconception.

A gambler, who refuses to accept the reality that they will lose in the long run, is driven by the hostility virus to continue until he/she proves to everyone that their gambling technique works. The major goal of carriers with this financial virus is to force the world to fit their view, no matter how much it may cost.

Do to others whatever you would like them to do to you. This is the essence of all that is taught in the law and the prophets. **Matthew 7:12**

The financial virus hostility supports the lust of the flesh by extorting money from its carriers and by encouraging them to purchase items they cannot afford as a reward.

Carriers of the financial virus of hostility usually reward themselves as a way to make their financial situation seem valid. God's children must hold onto their savings and learn to break the cycle of falling prey to the financial bondage of hostility immediately. Take this fight to another level and refuse to be victim to financial strongholds.

Keep watch and pray, so that you will not give in to temptation. For the spirit is willing, but the body is weak! **Matthew 26:41**

<u>Examples of how to win the battle of hostility:</u>

1. Stop using God's money to support movies that glorify hostility as a way to cope with stress.
2. Refuse to purchase another video game for your child that teaches them how to embrace hostility as a way of life.
3. Confess the peace of God over your inferiority complex.
4. Take better care of your finances and stop buying lunch everyday.
5. Beg the Holy Spirit for guidance and direction.
6. Register for a financial management class.
7. Stop impulse buying by reading the book "Emotional Intelligence" by Daniel Goleman and become a master of your own emotions.

Financial Stronghold #6: Outburst of Anger

Outburst of Anger is a financial virus used as a weapon to keep many in depression. Outburst of Anger will always be available as a confident supporter of the lust of the flesh.

A definition of anger is body tension: a view of the world as frustrating, insulting, unfair and/or assaulting. Outburst of anger is similar to wrath, a violent anger, full of rage. This financial virus once released can be very unkind and cruel to others. This kind of financial virus can be effective because it usually destroys property and is costly every time it shows up.

An individual who exhibits an outburst of anger is similar to someone taking poison and waiting for the other person to die. It will never happen. Outburst of anger is an attack that keeps God's children in financial bondage and if left untreated will kill its victims.

You must control your anger in order to fight this financial virus and win. Outburst of anger should not be used as a weapon to respond to bill collectors and loan officers. Responding to situations with this fleshly behavior is a sign of laying down arms and giving your enemies full access to your property.

The invisible financial war cannot be fought effectively by thinking in error that people owe you. You have created financial hell all by yourself, so boldly face all financial adversities that you consciously attracted into your life by supporting the lust of the flesh. Anger cannot protect you. Outburst of anger is designed to hurt both the carrier and its newly infected recipient. Carriers of this financial virus should seek God immediately for help.

Many workers go home crying each day due to mental, emotional and physical stress from their jobs. Thousands of dollars are being paid to psychologists to listen to individuals who run up huge bills by refusing to become financially responsible.

Monies that should be spent to see financial advisors have now provided a multi-billion dollar investment opportunity for anyone who designs new and more potent sleeping pills or a new drug that cannot cure our overspending habits.

Many individuals work long hours and get paid just enough to stay at their current job. Financial strongholds who hire these individuals understand as the workers desire to support the lust of the flesh intensifies, their desire to create a solution for release from financial bondage will diminish. So the cycle continues.

Don't befriend angry people or associate with hot-tempered people, or you will learn to be like them and endanger your soul. **Proverbs 22:24 & 25**

The primary reason for the use of outburst of anger is to get the opponent to give in to the demands of the financial virus carrier. For example, when an individual asks for a raise and the boss responds negatively to this request. To the boss asking for a raise is an injustice. The worker on the other hand retreats to working in an environment that spreads more viruses, reducing all chances of financial advancement.

On another level, the working poor usually allow themselves to be exposed to a work environment that spreads financial viruses such as: quarreling, hostility and outburst of anger as the perfect weapons to destroy many families.

Many work environments are often negative and toxic, releasing an unpleasant odor that workers take home to their spouse and children. Once the negative odor (virus) is release successfully into the home, family members begin to act out the same behaviors they experience in the workplace.

The invisible financial war is highly intensified in this industry where thousands of newly infected workers are enlisted hourly. The working poor allow themselves to be treated this way because of a consumer mentality. They want more things at all cost. No financial plans are necessary, just a constant willingness to work in an environment that supports their desire to have what they want no matter how painful to themselves, their children and their spouse.

Traits associated with carriers of the financial virus, outburst of anger, may include:
1. Increased likelihood of financial stress.
2. Job hopping.
3. Addiction to credit.
4. Loss of wages/income potential.
5. Greater difficulty in solving financial problems constructively.
6. A predisposition to overspend.

An angry person starts fights; a hot-tempered person commits all kinds of sin.
Proverb 29:22

Examples of how to win the battle against of outburst of anger:
1. Take the first step of recovery by registering for an anger management class.
2. Read books on how to handle anger more effectively.
3. Listen to the entire book of "Proverbs" 100 times.
4. Take a closer look at your reasons for personal sabotage. Could it be associated with your low self-worth?
5. Gather more knowledge about the enemy within. Take personal inventory and make changes to reflect the heart of Jesus Christ.
6. Practice self-control in all areas of your life. It is your life!
7. Learn to love yourself and others passionately.

Financial Virus Summary-Code Orange

Financial Virus #1
Quarreling: Quarreling is a financial virus that destroys families by reproducing itself: so as to strip individuals of all future savings and investments. Do not engage with anyone who starts an argument; it will cost you future savings.

Financial Virus #2
Hostility: Hostility is a financial virus that suppresses the truth. Infected individuals usually refuse physical evidence as truth. In order to win this financial war, simply face the truth about your financial situation and begin to pay your bills on time.

Financial Virus #3
Outburst of Anger: This financial virus, once released, can be very costly. The working poor are greatly affected by this virus. Take control of this financial virus by keeping your mouth shut when someone tries to engage you negatively.

Code Yellow

Financial Threat

Financial Stronghold #7: Jealousy

Jealousy is a financial threat used as a weapon to keep many wanting more.

Jealousy is a response to a threat that someone wants what you have. This financial threat does not have to be real, it could be imagined. The financial threat of jealousy usually works perfectly in the invisible realm producing a series of physical insecurities. In order to fight jealousy, you must see your negative relationship with money for what it is; a dissatisfaction with yourself.

The financial threat of jealousy is created first in the mind by individuals with insecurities. Once created, the financial threat becomes even more dangerous. Thoughts of constant fears and phobias regarding financial loss will increase until the imagined becomes real. You see, whatever you think about the most, you attract into your life. Financial loss is a fear for many; therefore threats have easy access to millions of minds who refuse to trust God with their finances.

Jealousy can be found in every culture. Many spend thousands of dollars to implement the best state of the art security systems in their homes and businesses. There are laws in place to protect our land and properties. Others purchase extra safety deposit boxes to hide jewelry, valuables and money as a way to protect material achievements.

The financial threat of jealousy keep many in constant fear of what someone will do to all the material things they have acquired by supporting the lust of the flesh. You need not fear the loss of anything. You do not own anything on this earth, you are a renter; it all belongs to God. You are only a steward (manger).

The financial threat of jealousy can be controlled by releasing yourself from the fear of loss. God's plan for your financial increase does not include jealousy. God's economic plan for your life is to become an effective manager with abundance and good health so as to enjoy the never ending increase he has in store for you. Being fearful is Satan's economic plan for unbelievers.

A competent and self-confident warrior is incapable of attracting the financial threat of jealousy. A self-confident warrior believes that God is their true source, and no weapons formed against them will prosper. The financial threat of jealousy is a mental cancer that must not be entertained, ever!

Anger is cruel, and wrath is like a flood, but jealousy is even more dangerous.
Proverbs 27:4

<u>Several ways to deal with the financial threats of jealousy may include:</u>

1. Replacing false beliefs about your financial situation with positive thoughts.
2. Identifying the reasons behind every thought of financial loss.
3. Understanding each emotion connected to thoughts of financial loss.
4. Communicating your feelings about financial loss on paper, with a pastor or close friend who is not under attack by the financial threat of jealousy.
5. Not denying the feelings of being threatened by this financial attack. Face this enemy head on and directly with the blood of Jesus and the Word of God.

For you are still controlled by your sinful nature. You are jealous of one another and quarrel with each other. Doesn't that prove you are controlled by your sinful nature? Aren't you living like people of the world? ***1 Corinthians 3:3***

<u>Examples of how to win the battle of jealousy:</u>

1. Be grateful for your present state/situation. Do not allow boredom to stimulate your lustful desires of pleasing the flesh.
2. Stop complaining. Seek the Kingdom of God first and everything else will be much easier for you.
3. Donate your overflow to the Salvation Army. You do not need so many shoes and clothes. Give away something you own every time the financial threat of jealousy shows up.
4. Ask God to bless and increase everyone you envy one thousand times more.
5. Use your own talent to create wealth for yourself. Know that overcoming jealousy is the Will of God for your life.
6. Refuse to embrace the loser mentality of supporting the lust of the flesh.
7. Create a list of strategies that you can use immediately to eliminate your jealousy of others; share your ideas with your financial mentor. Be proactive!

Financial Stronghold #8: Envy

Envy is a financial threat used as a weapon to keep God's children in the red.

The financial threat of envy is the desiring of another's trait, status, abilities, or worldly goods. This battle is motivated by the success of others. Envy is simply grudging others with the desire to have what they possess.

Envy is a major supporter of the lust of the flesh and is an effective threat because it teaches how to create personal identity using the material things of this world.

This financial threat resents the financial, spiritual or material gains of others. The success of others can produce great distress to an individual who is being attacked by the financial threat of envy. Envy is a sister to jealousy. Jealousy involves wanting to protect something (real or imagined) that you already have. Envy involves hating the success of others and wanting something they have.

Possible symptoms that the financial threat of envy has entered your life may include feelings of pain and anxiety when someone else:

1.   Drives a car you desire.
2.   Buys a home you would like.
3.   Spends money you wish you had.
4.   Travels to countries you love.
5.   Wears clothing that you think would look better on you.

The financial threat of envy is designed to be used directly by the intended victim. Hence the reason many college students become perfect targets. College students who buy things they do not need, and run up credit card debts without a job, only to impress people they do not like is a great indication that envy knows where your family lives.

Jessica Antle, a spokeswoman for MasterCard, said that one of the main reasons for a college student's debt is that credit cards are used for superficial and materialistic purposes.

Over the past several years, the financial threat of envy has gained high ground with college students. Studies have found that college students who live with a family household income of less than $50,000 are more likely than their peers to be in extreme credit card debt. The financial threat of envy must not be passed down to your children. God has given you the ability to create great abundance and wealth, not outrageous debt.

Then I observed that most people are motivated to success because they envy their neighbors. But this, too, is meaningless-like chasing the wind. **Ecclesiastes 4:4**

The financial threat of envy affects all levels of income. The goal of this financial stronghold is to create more and more trickery for its intended victim, so as to increase a higher level of distress for those who walk this way. Some institutions that are members of the financial threat team may include:

1. Casinos that provide endless ways (24hrs) to increase the appetite of your addictive behavior.

2. Credit-card companies who increase limits even though you are unable to pay off your current debt.

3. Department stores that constantly advertise hourly, daily, weekly or monthly sales to cater to the lie that you need another pair of shoes or a dress.

4. Banks that offers high interest loans to individuals who have bad credit and sometimes no stable income.

5. Colleges that offer financial aid to students to entice the desire of wanting more. This is the greatest financial tragedy ever. Most of these targeted victims often graduate with over $100,000 in debt and spend the rest of their lives making minimum payments on a loan that they could not afford when they began college.

6. Churches that talk about prosperity but do not bring in experts to teach members how to save and invest.

7. Churches that do not teach about prosperity, yet ask members to give offerings for new buildings, pastors, missions, and outreach funds. Members who give the most are usually received and treated better than those who cannot give. Hence the cycle of wanting something others have continues to grow like a disease within the church.

Don't worry about the wicked or envy those who do wrong. For like grass, they soon fade away. Like spring flowers, they soon wither. **Psalm 37:1,2**

Some Victims of Envy:

In L.A., on Thursday, another fight about gambling steeled Jueliene Butler's determination to leave her husband, as her children raced down the street on their bicycles and tricycles. The two shots that resounded through the neighborhood ended a tempestuous 26-year marriage between Rodney and Jueliene Butler in a murder-suicide heard by their 13-year-old daughter. *Source: Time Picayune 5/8/98*

ATLANTIC CITY—An unidentified man hanged himself under the Boardwalk on Thursday, the third suicide outside a casino in the last three months, police said. *Source: Associated Press 6/9/00*

A Long Island teen who had a "death wish" because of a $6,000 World Series gambling debt used a $1.75 toy gun to force cops to shoot and kill him, police said yesterday. *Source: New York Post 11/16/97*

A gambler, Robert Jewell, threatened to spray gunfire in an Elgin, Ill., casino, then returned home and shot himself. *Source: Los Angeles Times 6/22/97*

Kate, 40, a gambling addict and mother of 2, committed suicide by shooting herself in the head. *Source: St. Louis Post-Dispatch 2/22/95*

27-year old Larry ruined his career, maxed out his credit cards and finally killed himself after gambling away his girlfriend's rent money. *Source: TODAY 8/13/01*

My father, a successful lawyer in Los Angeles, was also a compulsive gambler, and he killed himself in 1976, shortly after one of his many trips to Las Vegas. *Source: Ward M. Winton St. Paul, Dec 1997*

"Almost all of my paycheck goes to pay off my credit cards," said Cindy, now 19 and a sophomore. "But once my credit card is paid off, I just max it out again."

*So don't be dismayed when the wicked grow rich and their homes become ever more splendid. For when they die, they take nothing with them. For their wealth will not follow them into the grave. **Psalm 49: 16,17***

Examples of how to win the battle of envy:

1. Create a savings plan for every financial goal. Refuse to purchase anything that you have not saved ahead of time for.

2. Assist one person daily to achieve his/her personal success. Sow a seed of kindness to help someone else succeed.

3. Attend an over spenders anonymous meeting in your community or start one.

4. Register with www.gam-anon.org to deal with gambling addiction. Save your money for projects that provide financial education programs for college students.

5. Accept your current financial state and create a plan for growth. Fall in love with saving for your future.

6. Do not purchase items on credit because of envy. Purchase items because you desire to please God and you have the cash to pay for them.

7. Liberate yourself by opening up a financial independent savings account today.

Financial Threat Summary-Code Yellow

Financial Threat #1

Jealousy: Jealousy is a response to a financial threat that someone wants what you have. There is no lack in God. Refuse to believe the lies being told about your self-worth and erase the financial threat that supports this lust of the flesh.

Financial Threat #2

Envy: The financial threat of envy is motivated by the success of others. Eliminate this financial threat in your life by developing and creating your own personal wealth.

Code White

Financial Emergency

Financial Stronghold #8: Idolatry

Idolatry is a financial emergency used as a weapon to corrupt God's children so as to keep them in constant need of aid. Idolatry reflects stubbornness and creates unrealistic relationships for those who view this fleshly behavior as a way to please God.

Idolatry is an effective financial stronghold because it takes away glory from God. Idolatry is a financial emergency that caters to the love or adoration of an idol and generally involves some form of ceremony/ritual. An idol is an image representing any symbol or object of devotion.

Forms of Idolatry:
 a. Worship of trees, rivers, hills, stones, etc.,
 b. Worshiping oneself
 c. Talent/Personal Ability Worship
 d. Hero Worship
 e. Worship of deceased ancestors
 f. Worship of cars, houses, clothing, food
 g. People Worship including pastors, priests, etc.

During a financial emergency many support the created object first, while God is offered second place. At times many work overtime looking for ways to increase income only to support the love for created objects. However, quite often there are no desires to work overtime to give a special offering to a family member who is trapped by poverty. God want to always be first in your life. God want all creation to honor him, by putting him first; not the things he made for you.

The public at large seems to know few boundaries when it comes to heaping adoration upon heroes. Top sports figures are able to earn millions of dollars per year because of the desire of the masses to see them perform. People are willing to pay enormous prices for tickets to get into events featuring these idols. In addition, billions of dollars are raised in advertising revenues due to the desire of the masses to watch sports on television. Source: Angelfire.com

Things not to worship: (Deuteronomy 4:15-19)
 1. So do not corrupt yourselves by making an idol in any form-whether of a man or a woman.
 2. An animal on the ground, a bird in the sky.
 3. A small animal that scurries along on the ground, or a fish in the deepest sea.
 4. And when you look up into the sky and see the sun, moon, stars-all the forces of heaven-don't be seduced into worshiping them. The Lord your God gave them to all the peoples of the earth.

So, my dear friends flee from the worship of idols. ***1 Corinthians 10:14***

The tendency to value something or someone in a way that hinders the love and trust owed to God can become very costly. Most of the time personal savings go towards purchasing items to be worshipped. You can save thousands of dollars just by cutting back in this area. Worshipping idols put God last. Eliminate idolatry spending in order to take control of this financial emergency that has a high probability of escalating.

Idolatry spending is just another form of low self-esteem. Individuals who practice these rituals are often rebellious and worship these items to feel better about their low levels of performance. Purchasing a car where you are always the only passenger is a form of idolatry. Buying a ticket to a ball game is a form of idolatry if you cannot give the same amount in an offering basket. Taking yourself to a restaurant and eating to the point of being sick is a form of idolatry.

Groups involved in dealing with financial emergencies effectively:

The Wisdom Center-Dr. Mike Murdock (teaches about wisdom being the principle thing for achieving financial freedom; call 1-817-759-0300 to order catalog)

Dr. Leroy Thompson-(teaches how to pull down the master strongholds off your finances, call 1-225-473-8874 to order products.)

Dr. Creflo Dollar-(teaches about breaking the spirit of poverty off your life, order products by visiting www.crefloministries.com)

Examples of how to win the battle of idolatry:

1. Create a list of things and people you currently worship and ask God to release you from idolatry.
2. Remove everything that interferes with your relationship with God and increase your prayer time.
3. Remove clutter around and in your house, car, and office and start your day with excitement. Money is not attracted to clutter and dirt, so keep your surroundings clean and watch financial opportunities flow much easier to you.
4. Stop trying to buy people's love and affection with God's money; give without checking to see if your gifts were received.
5. Use the money that you've saved to start your own successful business.
6. Fill up daily with the word of God, not on people or things.
7. Take control of your money by investing into mutual funds; visit www.sharebuilder.com to learn more about this industry, or visit your local library and check out books that will increase your financial wisdom.

Rebellion is as sinful as witchcraft, and stubbornness as bad as worshiping idols. So because you have rejected the command of the Lord, he has rejected you as King.
1 Samuel 15:23

Financial Stronghold #10: Sorcery

Sorcery is a financial emergency used to keep God's children as spending puppets. The ultimate purpose of the financial stronghold of sorcery is manipulation.

Sorcery sometimes known as magic is a conceptual system of thought, belief, and knowledge that asserts human ability through mystical and paranormal means. Sorcery covers items such as witchcraft, astrology, idol worship and endless deceptions in the name of providing a feeling that can only come from God. However, one of the greatest financial strongholds you will ever fight in this invisible war is against advertisers who use sorcery as a marketing tool.

You are under the influence of the financial stronghold of sorcery if you practice one or more of the following:
* Act helpless in taking care of yourself financially.
* Act incompetent when paying your bills.
* Throw temper tantrums when a bill collector calls your home.
* Lie about how much money you really have in the bank.
* Tell stories about your financial situation.
* Kiss up at work to get a raise.
* Blame others for your lack of savings.
* Exaggerate how much you are being paid.
* Act as if you are worthless.
* Act suicidal when cars, homes or furniture is being repossessed.

It is the job of most advertisers who practice sorcery to manipulate the behaviors of consumers to spend, spend, and spend. Sorcery is the best "con" game consumers will ever play with advertisers. Getting consumers to associate consumption with happiness is the greatest deception ever created. Many commercial advertisers focus on an individual's craving to please their fleshly desires, leading consumers to squander their immediate and future resources.

In the United States alone, in 2005, spending on advertising reached $144.32 billion, reported TSN Media Intelligence.

Advertising is a paid, one-way communication through a medium in which the manipulator is identified and the message is completely controlled by the manipulator. The goal is to saturate the mind of the intended consumer by delivering the manipulators' messages in every major medium including: television, radio, movies, magazines, newspapers, video games, flyers, postcards, the internet, and billboards. Sorcery advertisement promotes consumption, and many of God's children are being attacked severely with these messages through both the ears and eyes gate.

Worshiping foreign gods has sapped their strength, but they don't even know it.

Hosea 7:9

Many advertising clients are predominately profit generating corporations seeking to increase demand for their product or service by using the financial stronghold of sorcery.

The advertising industry is very large with an enormous potential for growth and needs more consumers in order to survive. You defeat the financial stronghold of sorcery by reducing your cravings to consume items you clearly do not need. Remember that God is not dead, he is alive, and there is victory for all those who choose Christ.

Television is generally considered the most effective format for manipulators where the high price television networks charge advertisers for commercial airtime during popular shows and games. The annual Super Bowl football game in the United States is known as much for its commercial advertisements as for the game itself. According to statistic, the average cost of a single, thirty second television spot during a Super Bowl game has reached $2.7 million (as of 2007.)

The accounting firm Price Water House and Coopers report projected worldwide advertising spending to exceed half-a-trillion dollars by 2010.

Money spent to support the financial stronghold of sorcery is astounding. There are many that seek out psychics and false spiritual leaders to fix their problems. In addition, these same individuals spend hundreds and sometimes thousand of dollars just to hear about their future. There are others who will not start their day without reading the astrological pages in the newspaper; while spending millions of dollars on books for their children that celebrate witches and warlords. There is no lack of support from the body of Christ for this financial stronghold. Fight back by being financially responsible with every dollar that comes through your hands. **Invest before spending.**

Why are so many churches promoting poverty? Why do so many Christians stay broke? Why are millions of children without an education fund? Why are Christians so obsessed with worshipping celebrity pastors? Could it be because they refuse to recognize that disobedience to the Lord has released a generational curse that continues to this day?

The financial stronghold of sorcery is a huge problem in the church. Refusing to follow God's economic plan is another way to promote poverty. Listen up people, open your eyes and take a good look at all the schemes being conjured up by sorcery to take personal savings and lead you, your family, and your friends towards a life that honors poverty and dishonor your birthright to prosperity. Oh yes! You are at war.

Do not listen to your false prophets, fortune-tellers, interpreters of dreams, mediums, and sorcerers. **Jeremiah 27:9**

<u>Examples of how to win the battle of sorcery</u>:

1. Stop calling the psychic hotlines; fall on your knees instead and cry out to Jesus Christ.
2. Read Psalm 91 to remove depression and stress; it is priceless.
3. Do not visit fortune-tellers; they are soldiers of the devil.
4. Do not entertain white or black magic. Entertain the love of Christ.
5. Stop purchasing books that glorify witches and warlords (use money to create a savings account for the celebration of your next birthday party.)
6. Remove all items from your home that do not glorify the Lord. Put it all in the trash!
7. Donate twenty-five percent of your income this month to your church declaring that you will no longer be a victim to this stronghold.

Financial Emergency Summary-Code White

Financial Emergency #1 (Idolatry)

Idolatry: Idolatry includes the worship of people and things. The financial stronghold of idolatry takes away Glory from God and must be eliminated by worshipping the creator of all things, not things he created.

Financial Emergency #2 (Sorcery)

Sorcery: Sorcery is a financial stronghold that manipulates through religion, witchcraft, fortune telling and advertising. The financial stronghold of sorcery can be blocked simply by creating an advertisement for yourself that manipulates **You** to save more and spend less.

Chapter Summary: The Attack (Financial Strongholds)

Code Green-Internal Financial Disasters

Selfish Ambition: Fight back by sharing your success and prosperity with others.

Dissension: Fight back through building synergistic partnerships.

Division: Fight back by allowing others to share their view and ideas with you.

Resource Books Available to Help with Selfish Ambition, Dissension, Division

(Checkout Google books, Amazon or Christianbooks.com to purchase your copy)
1. *Overcoming Negative Self-Image*—Author: Rick Joyner
2. *The Truth in the Mirror*—Author: Karla Downing
3. *The Joy of Conflict Resolution*—Author: Gary Harper

Code Orange-Financial Viruses

Quarreling: Fight back by keeping your mouth shut during times of disagreement.

Hostility: Fight back by facing the truth about your situation.

Outburst of Anger: Fight back by learning how to compromise.

Resource Books for Help with Quarreling, Hostility, Anger
(Checkout Google books, Amazon or Christianbooks.com to purchase your copy)
1. *Love: The Greatest Gift of All*—Author: Phyliss Le Peau
2. *Being the Person God Made You To Be*—Author: Joyce Meyer
3. *Anger & Stress Management, God's Way*—Author: Wayne Mack

Code Yellow-Financial Threats

Jealousy: There is no lack in God. The Lord is your shepherd, you lack nothing. Fight back by giving more.

Envy: Stop competing with your neighbors and allow God to create greatness through you. Fight back by celebrating the success of others.

Resource Books for Help with Jealousy and Envy
(Checkout Google books, Amazon or Christianbooks.com to purchase your copy)
1. *Overcoming Jealousy & Possessiveness*—Author: Paul Hauck
2. *Freedom from Addiction*—Author: Neil Anderson
3. *Overcoming the Spirit of Poverty*:—Author: Rick Joyner

Code White-Financial Emergencies
Idolatry: Fight back by giving God the Glory daily.
Sorcery: Fight back by refusing to be manipulated.

Resource Books for Help with Idolatry, Sorcery
(Checkout Google books, Amazon or Christianbooks.com to purchase your copy)
1. *Idolatry and the Hardening of the Heart*—Author: Edward Meadors
2. *Idols of the Heart*—Author: Elyse Fitzpatrick
3. *Spiritual Warfare*—Author: George Bloomer

The wicked in pride and arrogance hotly pursue and persecute the poor; let them be taken in the schemes which they have devised.

Psalm 10:2

Chapter Five

The Attack Part II
(Dirty Financial Secrets Exposed)

Chapter Outline—(Financial Codes)

Code Silver (Financial Terrorism)
#11 Drunkenness
#12 Wild Parties

Code Red (Financial Suicide)
#13 Lustful Pleasures

Code Blue (Eminent Financial Death)
#14 Impurity
#15 Sexual Immorality

Code Silver

Financial Terrorism

Financial Stronghold #11: Drunkenness

Drunkenness is an act of financial terrorism used to keep God's children in financial danger.

Drunkenness is a result of financial terrorism at its best. Drunkenness is a condition of being intoxicated by consumption of alcohol to a degree where physical faculties are affected. Excessive drinking of alcohol can control daily functions of an individual, thereby creating a dependency on the substance and pulling them away from receiving the love of God. Drunkenness is very profitable for the alcohol industry. However, this financial stronghold is elated by the large sums of money available from underage and abusive drinkers.

According to new research in the U.S. the underage drinking market is making the alcohol industry nearly $23 billion dollars a year. Research also states that alcohol abuse and addiction costs the nation an estimated $220 billion in 2005; more than cancer ($196 billion) and obesity ($133 billion.)

Individuals affected by the financial stronghold of drunkenness may include one or more of the following:

1. Believing alcohol is necessary to have fun.
2. Lying about how much alcohol he or she is consuming.
3. Getting drunk on a regular basis.
4. Stealing from friends and family members to support the addiction of drunkenness.
5. Experiencing blackouts; forgetting what he or she did while drinking.
6. Frequent hangovers.
7. Problems at work or getting in trouble with the law.

Alcohol Calculator (Sample)

Type of Drink	Cost per Bottle	Weekly Intake	Annual Savings Lost
Wine	$20	1	$1040
Gin	$21	1	$1092
Vodka	$19	1	$988
Beer	$3	7	$1092
Whiskey	$18	1	$936
Rum	$14	1	$728

The total economic cost for alcohol related crashes cost $46 Billion.
Source: Luhs.org

Drunkenness and anguish will fill you, for your cup is filled to the brim with distress and desolation, the same cup your sister Samaria drank. **Ezekiel 23:33**

Successful dealers that support the financial stronghold of drunkenness may include one or more of the following:

1. Sports Bars
2. Pubs
3. Dance Clubs
4. Casinos
5. Happy Hour
6. Receptions
7. Weddings
8. Pool Halls
9. Country and Western Bars
10. Pizza Parlors
11. Bowling Alleys
12. College Hangouts
13. Country Clubs
14. Hotel Bars
15. Amusement Parks serving Alcohol
16. Racing Tracks
17. Baseball Parks
18. Comedy Clubs
19. Boat Marinas
20. Restaurants that serve Alcohol
21. Places that people go after the bars are closed
22. Friends and Family members who offer alcohol as a welcome

According to statistics, 70% of attempted suicides involve frequent alcohol and other drug use. The financial stronghold of drunkenness produces addicts. Once the intended victim becomes addicted, he/she becomes a member with the many others who are in bondage and completely dependent on alcohol as their savior.

In addition, the addict's thoughts, ideas, desires and behaviors are soon dominated by a stronghold that cares nothing about the individual's happiness. This stronghold cares only about taking all financial resources and leading each victim straight to hell.

Watch out! Don't let your hearts be dulled by carousing and drunkenness, and by the worries of this life. Don't let that day catch you unaware, like a trap. For that day will come upon everyone living on the earth. **Luke 21:34**

Examples of how to win the battle of drunkenness:

1. Volunteer with organizations that assist drunk drivers with their lack of control. Use this as a chance to help someone else win their life back.

2. Donate to Alcoholics-Anonymous.org (AA is a fellowship of men and women who share their experiences, strengths and hope with each other, so they can solve their common problem and help others to recover from alcoholism. AA's purpose is to help former addicts stay sober and help alcoholics achieve sobriety.)

3. Teach your children to become emotionally strong early. Teach positive ways of dealing with stress and anxiety. Read Proverbs to your children, and provide them with options that are constructive, not destructive.

4. Save all finances used to support this industry and create a brilliant education program for teens to learn the value of life without alcohol.

5. Do not be afraid to ask for help. Refuse to be in bondage any longer and reach out to the individuals that God put in your life for comfort and support.

6. Strive to win this battle without being forced behind bars. Don't wait until you take the life of a friend or a stranger. Get help before it's too late.

7. Meet with a friend, pastor or counselor weekly to discuss the reasons behind your drinking. Face all demonic thoughts about your past. Believe God has given you victory over the financial stronghold of alcohol.

Happy is the land whose king is a noble leader and whose leaders feast at the proper time to gain strength for their work, not to get drunk. **Ecclesiastes 10:17**

Financial Stronghold #12: Wild Parties

Wild Parties are an act of financial terrorism used to gather God's children to the slaughter house right before the massacre begins.

In today's society wild parties are being used as the perfect hideout to commit financial terrorism amongst God's children. It is surprising how many individuals who are trapped and unaware of how the financial stronghold of wild parties steals their future savings simultaneously and eventually their lives.

Participating in the wild party atmosphere is a rising epidemic for many families. Billions of dollars are being made annually from the trafficking of legal and illegal drugs to keep these parties going. For example, American consumers spend billions of dollars on prescription and designer drugs each year, most of which is being used at these parties.

Wild parties are perfect breeding grounds for financial terrorism. Most wild parties are not submitted to discipline or control; hence, the introduction of one of the most deadly financial strongholds: legal and illegal drugs. The legal and illegal drug trade is the financial engine that fuels the lifestyle of many individuals who have turned their back on God.

Legal and illegal drugs may cause one or more of the following to their victims:
a.   Disruption to the brain chemistry
b.   Seizures or heart attacks
c.   Death
d.   Increased violence
e.   Long-term damage to parts of the brain critical to thought and memory
f.   Respiratory problems
g.   Dependency
h.   Impaired perception
i.   Diminished short-term memory
j.   Loss of concentration and coordination
k.   Anxiety, panic attacks, and paranoia
l.   Hallucinations
m.   Damage to the reproductive and immune system
n.   Increase risk of cancer
o.   Impaired judgment

In November 2004, a United Nations Security Council report described "terrorism" as any act intended to cause death or serious bodily harm to civilians or non-combatants. Judging from the list above, there is probable cause to conclude that hard earned money being spent on drugs to keep these wild parties going is a definite form of terrorism. Remember, this is war. The attacks are deadly; you must turn to God.

Each act of financial terrorism committed is a performance devised to have an impact on a larger audience. Much of the time, the victims of financial terrorism are targeted not because they are threats, but because they are clueless as to the dangers awaiting them at these wild parties. Victims of financial terrorism usually support the lust of the flesh by doing whatever comes to mind without restrictions. In addition, victims of financial terrorism believe they are invincible and believe they know what is best. These victims want nothing to do with God.

"I use to be so cool," Erin told us in "Voice of the Victims" a film produced and directed by Beth Pearce. That was before Erin took the drug Ketamine and quickly fell to the floor, convulsing. Even though paramedics responded quickly, Erin's heart was stopped for 17 minutes, halting the flow of blood to the brain of this delightful and intelligent young woman." Stand against this stronghold with confidence.

Financial terrorists usually disguise themselves and hide among their intended victims. They also fight from the midst of their victims, posing as a solution to a problem. America's war on drug uses a similar disguise.

Those labeled as financial terrorists rarely identify themselves as so; and typically use other terms such as:

   a.   Doctors
   b.   Politicians
   c.   Chemists
   d.   Health Care Providers
   e.   Business Man/Women
   f.   Insurance Policy Makers
   g.   Non-Profit and many more

The U.S. Federal government spent over $19 billion dollars in 2004 on the War on Drugs, a rate of about $600 per second. The budget has since been increased by over a billion dollars. Source: Office of National Drug Control Policy

   *   How is it possible that America is still plagued by this demon?
   *   Why are so many teenagers gaining access to underage wild parties with drugs as the main choice of activity?
   *   Where are the parents of these children with billions of dollars to support the drug industry? Are they being attacked as well?
   *   Whose fault is it that in the year 2008 both legal and illegal drug makers has become champions at financial terrorism?
   *   Is it America's fault?
   *   Is it the drug dealers fault?
   *   Could it be that many are still blinded to this invisible financial war?

According to statistics, some of the favorite drugs being sold at wild parties to steal future savings include one or more of the following:

1. Ecstasy is a drug closely related to methadrine and popular because it typically creates in the user an illusion of warmth, closeness and compatibility. Before it was made illegal in 1985, it was used by psychiatrists as a therapeutic tool.

2. Ketamine also known as K. Special K or Vitamin K. was originally created for use as a human anesthetic, and is still being used as a general anesthetic for children. This drug is also used as an animal tranquilizer by veterinarians. It is also a strong hallucinogenic drug that impairs perceptions, increases feelings of euphoria and distorts the user sense of time and place.

3. GHB is an odorless and tasteless liquid. GHB was originally developed as a sleep aid. One dose can impair motor coordination by as much as six drinks of alcohol. A capful will make you feel intoxicated, but two capfuls could be fatal.

4. DXM replaced codeine as the primary active ingredient of cough suppressants on the market in an attempt to bring down codeine dependency.

5. Speed was used legally for decades for nasal congestion, weight control, mild depression, and to stay alert. Now it is being produced as an illegal drug. Speed users are at higher HIV and hepatitis risk because of unsafe sex and needle sharing.

6. Marijuana, according to American Council for Drug Education reduces learning ability and limits the capacity to absorb and retain information. Marijuana is also considered to be the world's most dangerous drug.

7. Steroid is big business for the sports industry. Athletes spend thousands of dollars just to experience visions from their limited imagination of being superman or superwoman. A steroid is a drug used to increase muscle mass, strength and endurance. It is also linked to liver tumors, heart damage, high blood pressure and high death rate.

But why do you indulge that Balaam crowd? Don't you remember that Balaam was an enemy agent, seducing Balak and sabotaging Israel holy pilgrimage by throwing unholy parties? **Revelation 2:14-15**

<u>Examples of how to win the battle of wild parties</u>:

1. Gain an advantage by using the money you do not spend for wild parties to help build homes for the elderly.
2. Increase your Financial Intelligence. Read books on finance; attend seminars that teach how to grow wealth.
3. Face your loneliness by turning your life completely over to God.
4. Enroll in a one year discipleship program with the Dream Center. The Dream Center offers discipleship programs for adult men, women and a teen program for both girls and boys. From helping with drug and alcohol recovery, to providing spiritual-based counseling to working through issues of anger or emotional struggles, the Dream Center's program is a live-in, work-discipline based, intensive one year program. Visit the website www.dreamcenter.org for more information.
5. Contact Beth Pearce at www.voiceofthevictims.com to see how you can help families who are victims of this drug war.
6. Organize a family barbeque and have fun.
7. Become more responsible with your time: Choose to live.

Financial Terrorism Summary-Code Silver

Financial Terrorism #1 (Drunkenness)

Drunkenness: Drunkenness is a result of financial terrorism at its best. Drunkenness steals lifetime savings. Underage and abusive drinkers are perfect targets. Create a plan to fight the financial stronghold of drunkenness by supporting a local AA chapter.

Financial Terrorism #2 (Wild Parties)

Wild Parties: Wild parties are perfect breeding grounds for financial terrorism. Legal and illegal drug trafficking at these parties often produces great harm to those who are looking for a way to feel better about their separation from God. Fight this financial stronghold by educating yourself, family and friends about the dangers awaiting those who turn their back on the Lord.

Code Red

Financial Suicide

Financial Stronghold #13: Lustful Pleasures

Lustful pleasures are the easiest financial stronghold used to lure God's children towards a slow and easy death.

Lustful pleasures are any intense desire or craving for self-gratification. Lustful pleasures take focus off what God thinks about you to what you think about yourself. Lustful pleasures such as a lust for money, power or food are the greatest financial strongholds to seduce God's children in their quest to commit financial suicide.

Catering to your lustful pleasures refuses all financial wisdom and unconsciously welcome financial suicide. Many individuals who live to please themselves are no longer interested in how their behavior will affect God or others; however Satan wants desperately for these individuals to fulfill each lustful pleasure that has taken up residence in their hearts.

Financial suicide is an **intentional act** of terminating your savings by spending more than what you earn to support the lust of the flesh.

Warning signs of Financial Suicide:
a. Poor saving habits
b. Spending more than intended at the grocery store
c. Purchasing items solely to keep up with neighbors
d. Bribing people for a better position
e. Purchasing every new diet pill that hits the market
f. Eating for emotional support
g. Loss of sleep due to financial stress and worry
h. Giving with the intention of controlling others
i. Purchasing more than one cup of coffee or latte daily
j. Shopping without a list
k. Thoughts about lack of money, food, and power

The lust for food costs many Americans their health. Millions of individuals willingly spend their weekly savings to support their lust for food. Obesity is at an all time high in both children and adults due to their intense desire to consume more food than necessary.

Eating is a pleasurable experience for most people, but for some, eating is an addiction. An eating addiction is the forcing of oneself to eat too much. Hence we have gluttony.

Gluttony is the perfect word to describe the lust for food. Gluttony is the overindulgence and over consumption of food or drink to the point of waste, resulting in a large sum of money going down the drain.

Lust for money is a common issue in many cultures. Family time is non-existent and spiritual time is completely forgotten by those pursing money as their

God. The amount of time spent at work has increased over the last decade giving birth to workaholics.

Workaholics don't believe in quitting at the end of the day or balancing work with God, family, and health. Workaholics view their jobs as the most important thing and are driven to serve money as their God.

There is a battle which is gaining high ground among those who lack financial wisdom; they are called the working poor. The working poor is a term used to describe individuals and families with a college/university degree, who maintain regular employment, yet remain in poverty due to low levels of pay and high expenses.

The working poor usually work to pay their bills but create a negative net worth due to their inability to fight this financial war and win. They are victims of a war they do not even know exists.

The goal of this financial stronghold is to convince victims that working excessively for money is the only way to succeed. However, this false statement is born from the pit of hell. You were not created for money. Money was created as a tool for you to display God's greatness. A carpenter must control (subdue) all his tools and use it wisely so as to achieve success with each building. God's children are commanded to rule (subdue) money so as to bring Glory to God.

Money is designed to go to work and produce increase, via savings, investments, etc. God created money for you to enjoy, just like he created beautiful cars, homes, family, friends, the sun, the moon, the stars, all for your enjoyment.

You are not created to serve anything or anyone except God. The lust for money rules over many because there is no love for God in their heart. Lusting for money is a definite form of financial suicide.

Lust for money signs to look for:
   a.   Working during the holidays
   b.   Working overtime every week
   c.   Always the last to leave work
   d.   Desk piled high with assignments to keep you busy during the weekends
   e.   No time for God
   f.   No time for family
   g.   No time for exercise
   h.   No time for relaxation
   i.   Purchase expensive gifts for children as a form of parenting
   j.   Lack of sleep due to too much work

Let your character or moral disposition be free from love of money and be satisfied with your present circumstances and with what you have for He Himself has said, I will not in any way fail you nor give you up nor let you down. **Hebrews 13:5**

The lust for power is simply a desire to gain control over others. In order to gain control over others, one must have control over the things that others desire or need.

Billions of dollars are being spent annually on drugs, alcohol, and food, while the lust for power increases. As demand increases for consumption, so does the lust of power to control distribution. An example can be seen very clearly in the oil industry.

The lust for more petroleum globally is just beginning. As China grows wealthier, so does their desire for increased oil consumption! Americans went from $1.99 per gallon for oil to paying over $4.00 per gallon at the pump overnight because there are no alternatives to reduce prices. Lust for power in the oil industry is evil in its worst kind leading victims daily towards suicide.

American politicians have dominated the world with news about increased threats from Iraq and terrorism; however, until today there has been no physical plan implemented by either party to produce effective solutions for Americans to reduce their dependency on foreign oil.

In his newly published memoirs, Alan Greenspan, former chairman of the Federal Reserve said, "I'm saddened that it is politically inconvenient to acknowledge what everyone already knows-the Iraq war is largely about oil."

The lust for power is designed to eventually kill all those who run after it. God's children must learn to care for each other and treat neighbors with kindness and love. There is more than enough power for everyone to experience. There is no lack on God's earth. Creating more situations that support the error thinking of lack will only increase the desire to gain control over others, which inevitably will produce financial suicide.

For the world offers only a craving for physical pleasure, a craving for everything we see, and pride in our achievements and possessions. These are not from the Father, but are from this world. **1 John 2:16**

<u>Examples of how to win the battle of lustful pleasures:</u>

1. Spend time meeting the needs of your family members, friends, community etc.
2. Run for a political office and win so as to become a voice from God.
3. Set challenging goals that will help to reduce your lack of inner peace.
4. Set a goal to create a solution for the lust for food, money and power.
5. Declare daily that you have personal power; therefore you do not need to control anyone.
6. Ask God to renew your mind daily; seek his face for contentment.
7. Ask God to remove all unrighteous behavior. Everything that is not of God, ask him to remove it today.
8. Add up all the money you have spent within the past month on lustful pleasures and sow twice that amount into the Benny Hinn Ministry (a healing ministry for the nation-www.bennyhinn.org) declaring that you are completely free from all lustful behaviors and thoughts.

Financial Suicide Summary-Code Red

Financial Suicide: Lustful Pleasures

Lustful pleasures are any intense desire or craving for self-gratification. Lust for food, money or power can become a critical state for many. Win this battle by believing there is more than enough for everyone on the planet. There is no scarcity, only abundance.

Code Blue

Eminent Financial Death

Financial Stronghold #14: Impurity

Impurity is a financial stronghold that keeps God's children in bondage while preparing them for hell. Spending your income just to steal glances at porn magazines or to purchase items to enhance the practice of masturbation are the greatest forms of slavery to the flesh.

Impurity is a desire; wish or intention to do something that is immoral. Individuals attacked by this financial stronghold are usually left feeling dirty, unworthy, broke, guilty, and ashamed of the impure act or thought about what they've committed.

Erotica and sexual themes continue to be big business in our society every year. Sex appeal is used widely to sell jewelry, cars, jeans, and even toothpaste. Sexy is now considered to be acceptable in children's clothing and toys. No wonder we have trouble with thoughts of impurity.

Due to the overwhelming offers of sexual stimulations from advertisers (manipulators), sex is promoted on buses, billboards, magazines, and at the movies. Wherever we go, there is an over abundance of sexual advertisements that prepares society for a massacre. Advertisement laced with sexual connotations often leaves subliminal messages that when ingested over and over will cause the audience to fall prey to the idea that impurity is good. Saturation does work!

There are countless books and movies to rent and buy that promote impure messages going against the Will of God. Many of the messages promoted by manipulators (advertisers) usually support other financial strongholds such as adultery, selfishness, deceit, lust, and many more. Impure messages deposited into your spirit through books, videos and movies help to formulate impure thoughts which eventually lead to acts of impurity.

Don't you realize that those who do wrong will not inherit the Kingdom of God? Don't fool yourselves. Those who indulge in sexual sin, or who worship idols, or commit adultery, or are male prostitutes, or practice homosexuality, or thieves, or greedy people, or drunkards, or are abusive, or cheat people-none of these will inherit the Kingdom of God. Some of you were once like that. But you were cleansed; you were made holy; you were made right with God by calling on the name of the Lord Jesus Christ and by the Spirit of our God. **1 Corinthians 6:9, 10 &11**

Many Christians and non-Christians donate billions of dollars annually to an industry that exploits every kind of sexual sin that can be conceived in the mind. Money that should be used to spread the gospel is being used daily to fund programs such as pornography and sexually immoral materials and activities on the internet at the speed of light.

Because we belong to the day, we must live decent lives for all to see. Don't participate in the darkness of wild parties and drunkenness, or in sexual promiscuity and immoral living, or in quarreling and jealousy. **Romans 13:13**

Sexuality is considered to be one of the most powerful tools for marketing products or services to the public. Sex sells and can be very effective for attracting immediate interest for those who are slaves to impurity. The only way to have control over your life and finances is to surrender completely all your thoughts to God, asking him to release you from the bondage of immorality.

Because of the weakness of your human nature, I am using the illustration of slavery to help you understand all this. Previously, you let yourselves be slaves to impurity and lawlessness, which led ever deeper into sin. Now you must give yourselves to be slaves to righteous living so that you will become holy. **Romans 6:19**

At 12 billion dollars a year, the revenues of the porn industry in the U.S are bigger than the NFL, NBA and Major League Baseball combined. Worldwide porn sales reported to be 57 billion dollars. To put this in perspective, Microsoft, who sells the operating system used on most of the computers in the world (in addition to other software), reported sales of 36.8 billion dollars in 2004. (Source: Family Safe Media)

Outside the city are the dogs-the sorcerers, the sexual immoral, the murderers, the idol worshipers, and all who love to live a lie. **Revelation 22:15**

"Last year, Comcast, the nation's largest cable company, made over $50 million from adult programming. All the nation's top cable operators, from Time Warner to Cablevision, distribute sexually explicit material to their subscribers. But you won't read about it in their annual reports. Same with satellite providers like EchoStar and DirecTV, which is owned by Hughes Technology, a subsidiary of General Motors. How much does DirecTV make off adult products? "They don't break the number out. But I would guess they'd probably get a couple hundred million, maybe as much as $500 million, of adult entertainment, in a broad sense," says Denise McAlpine, a partner in McAlpine Associates, who has tracked the entertainment industry for over two decades. (Source: CBS News Special Report, November 2003)

You can be sure that no immoral, impure, or greedy person will inherit the Kingdom of Christ and of God. For a greedy person is an idolater, worshipping the things of this world. **Ephesians 5:5**

"The porn industry employs an excess of 12,000 people in California. In California alone the porn industry pays over $36 million in taxes every year." (Source: Bill Lyon, a former lobbyist for the defense industry turned lobbyist for porn, as quoted by CBS News November 2003)

For all nations have drunk the wine of her passionate unchastity, and the rulers and leaders of the earth have joined with her in committing fornication, and the business men of the earth have become rich with the wealth of her excessive luxury and wantonness. **Revelation 18:3**

Masturbation has always been an invisible subject for many Christians; however, we need to address this issue because it involves our finances, thoughts, mind, body and spirit. If the body is the temple of the Lord, why do many commit such detestable acts of selfishness with it? Why do God's children spend hard earned money to buy trashy magazines and sex toys that drive them farther away from God?

Masturbation refers to sexual stimulation. Masturbation affects your sexuality and can become addictive. With so much abundance of love available from the true loving God, it makes no sense for God's children to defile themselves with the animalistic behavior of masturbation.

Sexual fantasy is adultery. One cannot experience a healthy marriage while each partner takes personal pleasure breaks. If you are married and find yourself struggling with this issue, there is help for you. (See the reference books below.)

Many people struggle with the financial bondage of impurity and that is why so many relationships die from sickness and disease in the end. Impurity has severe consequences because it disrespects the temple of the Holy One.

Sexual expression between a man and a woman in the context of marriage should be sacred. The practice of impurity is not worth loosing your whole family. It is not worth it for you to work hard to give money to lawyers because you refuse to obey God's law in Matthew 5:27-28 which states "Thou shalt not commit adultery."

Statistically, the more sexually involved you are before marriage, the more likely you are to commit adultery after marriage, (Source: Andrew M. Greeley, Faithful Attraction: Discovering Intimacy, Love and Fidelity in American Marriage (New York: Tom Doherty Associates, 1991)

And don't forget Sodom and Gomorrah and their neighboring towns, which were filled with immorality and every kind of sexual perversion. Those cities were destroyed by fire and serve as a warning of the eternal fire of God's judgment. **Jude 1:7**

Children of the most High God are in agreement today and speak boldly against the porn industry in the Name of Jesus. I rebuke every demonic force that supports all users, developers, customers and beneficiaries of this industry. I come in agreement right now with every child of the living God to declare that everyone who is a member of this industry will bow down to Jesus Christ, turn from their wicked ways and choose to build schools, churches and hospitals for the greater good of all mankind. I come in agreement with fellow brothers and sisters from the four corners of the earth and declare that the souls of every member in this industry, their friends, their families and their descendants belong to Jesus Christ today. Amen!

Examples of how to win the battle of impurity:
1. Repent every time your mind wanders to an impure thought. Don't be afraid to repent knowing God will give you strength to be faithful to your spouse.
2. Live a life that is holy and acceptable to the Lord Jesus Christ. Refuse to watch certain movies or read books that promote sexually immorality.
3. Take action by visiting xxxchurch.com. This Christian website provides a series of self-help programs for anyone who really wants to break this negative attraction to the flesh.
4. Confess Romans 10:9&10. Receive Jesus Christ as Lord and Savior. Give thanks for Salvation each day.
5. Support the National Law Center for Children and Families in their fight against porn www.nationallaecenter.org 3819 Plaza Drive, Fairfax, VA 22030-2512 (703) 691-4626
6. Contact the Ed Young Ministries to receive prayer to break the financial stronghold of impurity in your life. For more information visit www.edyoung.com
7. Choose to think like Christ. Listen to the Bible on CD daily! This simple act will wash your mind and prepare you for a Holy day.

*Let there be no sexual immorality, impurity, or greed among you. Such sins have no place among God's people. **Ephesians 5:3***

Financial Stronghold #15 Sexual Immorality

Sexual Immorality is a financial stronghold that brings death to all followers.

Sexual immorality is currently at an all time high. Adultery is no longer a sin according to many. Incest is ok in some families. Rent a husband/wife is now competing with swapping. How could we be so blind to the list of sexual sins commanded clearly by God in Leviticus 18 that bring death?

The easiest addiction to develop is sexual addiction. Due to unmet desires and unhealthy ways of dealing with stress, many have become reliant on sexual addiction as the only way to cope.

Sexual addiction is an abnormal use of our sex drive. Individuals who are addicted to sex usually twist a beautiful experience between a husband and a wife to include pictures, strangers, children and even animals.

God commanded in Leviticus that we should not live like the people in Egypt. Choose life by obeying God's laws. Polluting yourself with acts of sexual immorality is a demonic force that will take your life. Death to all who come this way!

Sexual Immoral acts to stay away from as commanded by God include:

a. Sex with a close relative
b. Sex with your father and mother
c. Sex with your father's wife
d. Sex with your sister or step sister
e. Sex with your son's daughter or daughter's daughter
f. Sex with your aunt or uncle
g. Sex with daughter in law or son in law
h. Sex with your brother's wife
i. Sex with your sister's husband
j. Sex with both a woman and her daughter or granddaughter
k. Sex with your wife's sister while she is living
l. Sex with a woman during the time of her menstrual period
m. Sex with your neighbor's wife
n. Sex with a man as one does with a woman
o. Sex with an animal

I can hardly believe the report about the sexual immorality going on among you-something that even pagans don't do. I am told that a man in your church is living in sin with his stepmother. **1 Corinthians 5:1**

Out of eighty pastors surveyed, 98% had been exposed to porn, 43% intentionally accessed a sexually explicit website. (Source: National Coalition survey of pastors. Seattle. April 2000)

Sexual immorality is a global issue. This demonic force grows stronger as we move away from the teachings of God. In the Middle East, husbands are allowed to leave their wives on the weekends to participate in pleasurable time with prostitutes. The amount of money being wasted for pleasure affects the entire world.

The World Bank estimates that rape and domestic abuse account for five percent of healthy years of life lost to women of reproductive age in developing countries.

In China, there is an alarming amount of children who are being used as sex slaves for business men who travel from all over the world to satisfy their sexual desires. Thanks to a boldly increasing economy, sex is China's biggest business. The country that supplies 70% of the world's sex toys finds itself right in the middle of a financial war that has already brought death to millions of families globally. God is not pleased with these statistics and encourages those of us who are trapped to turn away from sexually immorality and seek holiness **NOW!**

Run from sexual sin! No other sin so clearly affects the body as much as this one does. For sexual immorality is a sin against your own body. **1 Corinthians 6:18**

In Africa, sexual abuse and violence is frequently directed towards females and youth who lack the economic and social status to resist or avoid it. Money spent to cure sexual diseases in Africa now exceeds money spent to provide food for families with limited education on how to become financially independent.

In India, young women may experience abuse in the forms of rape, sexual assault, sexual exploitation and female genital mutilation. Husbands in India are willing to pay doctors to have their female children aborted instead of using the money for the financial education of their young girls and boys.

In America, sexual predators find expensive and innovative ways to lure children into gruesome sexual behaviors often times ending in death. Sexual predators have more rights than most criminals in America. This war respects no one. We are all targets, so get strong, or get beaten.

How many more lives will you allow this demonic force to take before you wake up and begin to take responsibility? God so loved the world that he gave his only begotten Son, that whosoever believes might be saved from this horrible and heart wrenching lifestyle. God loves you dearly and wants you to invite him into daily activities so that he can protect you from the evils of this world.

Don't you realize that you become the slave of whatever you choose to obey? You can be a slave to sin, which leads to death, or you can choose to obey God, which leads to righteous living. **Romans 6:16**

Examples of how to win the battle of sexual immorality:

1. God's forgiveness covers all your sins; so repent today and receive God's Glory.
2. Save your life by refusing to give your money to prostitutes. Give it to the work of God instead!
3. Do not fear your past, there is hope for everyone. Ask one of God's powerful disciples to pray with you.
4. Add up all the money you have already spent on sex toys and porn magazines, double the amount, and give it as a donation to rape victims.
5. When visiting online chat rooms, declare to your audience that the devil is a liar and you are completely cured from all sexual immoralities in the name of Jesus.
6. Begin or join a support group for those who desire to win this battle for themselves, family and friends.
7. Help destroy this financial stronghold by sowing a monthly seed to TBN (Christian Television) www.tbn.org to help spread the Gospel to the nations.

Eminent Financial Death Summary-Code Blue

Eminent Financial Death #1 (Impurity)
Impurity: Impurity is a desire, wish or intention to do something that is immoral. Many Christians and non-Christians donate billions of dollars annually to an industry that exploits every kind of sexual sin that can be conceived in the mind. Fight back by aligning with individuals and organizations who have demonstrated great success against this demon.

Eminent Financial Death #2 (Sexual Immorality)
Sexual Immorality: Sexual immorality is currently at an all time high. Sex is the easiest addiction to develop and has brought death to millions of families. Get ready; pick up your defensive and offensive spiritual weapons (listed in the following chapters) and move forward to victory over sexual immorality.

*Instead, clothe yourself with the presence of the Lord Jesus Christ. And don't let yourself think about ways to indulge your evil desires. **Romans 13:14***

Chapter Summary: The Attack (Financial Strongholds)

Code Silver—Financial Terrorism

Drunkenness: Drunkenness steals lifetime savings. Underage and abusive drinkers are perfect targets. Teach the Word of God to your children. Fight back by learning effective mind and stress management skills.

Wild Parties: Wild parties are perfect breeding grounds for financial terrorism. Legal and illegal drug trafficking at these parties often produce great harm to those who are looking for a way to feel better about their separation from God. Seek God for protection. Fight back by saying no to the things of this world.

Resource Books for Help with Drunkenness, Wild Parties
(Checkout Google books, Amazon or Christianbooks.com to purchase your copy)
1. *Divine Intervention*—Author: Mark Shaw
2. *90 Days, One Day at a Time*—Author: John Behnke
3. *Drinks Without Alcohol*—Author: Jane Brandt

Code Red-Financial Suicide

Lustful Pleasures: Lustful pleasures are any intense desire or cravings for self-gratification. Lust for food, money or power are critical states for anyone. Developing a generosity spirit will immediately slow down this enemy. Fight back by developing a desire to please God.

Resource Books for Help with Lustful Pleasures
(Checkout Google books, Amazon or Christianbooks.com to purchase your copy)
1. *Change Your Heart, Change Your Life*—Author: Gary Smalley
2. *Seeking the Face of God*—Author: Gary Thomas
3. *Conquering Your Hidden Kingdoms—Author: Rocky Morris*

Code Blue-Eminent Financial Death

Impurity: Impurity is a desire, wish or intention to do something that is immoral. Pornography and masturbation open the doors to hell. Stay away! Fight back by renewing your mind with the Word of God.

Sexual Immorality: Sex is the easiest addiction to develop and has brought death to millions of families. Seek God now and stop your family from being next in line. Fight back by forgiving those who introduced you to this industry.

Resource Books for Help with Impurity
(Checkout Google books, Amazon or Christianbooks.com to purchase your copy)
1. *The Way of Purity: Enjoying Lasting Freedom in Christ* Author: Mike Cleveland
2. *The Secret in the Pew: Pornography in the Lives of Christian Men-Breaking the Bondage of Sexual Sin* Author: David Blythe
3. *The Pornography Trap: Setting Pastors and Laypersons Free From Sexual Addiction* Author: Ralph Earle
4. *Think Before You Look! 40 Powerful Reasons to Avoid Pornography* Author: Daniel Henderson

Resource Books for Help with Sexual Immorality
(Checkout Google books, Amazon or Christianbooks.com to purchase your copy)
1. *Healing Wounds of Sexual Addiction* Author: Mark Laaser
2. *Sex: A Pocket Bible Study & Journal* Author: Hayley Dimarco
3. *Every Young Woman's Battle: Guarding Your Mind, Heart, and Body in a Sex-Saturated World* Author: Shannon Ethridge
4. *Love, Sex, and Lasting Relationships: God's Prescription for Enhancing Your Love Life* Author: Chip Ingram
5. *God's Design for Sex Series* Author: Carolyn Nystrom

Financial Warfare Prayer
1 Chronicles 16:8-36

Give thanks to the Lord and proclaim his greatness.
    Let the whole world know what he has done.
Sing to him; yes, sing his praises.
    Tell everyone about his wonderful deeds.
Exult in his holy name;
    Rejoice, you who worship the Lord.
Search for the Lord and for his Strength;
    continually seek him.
Remember the wonders he has performed,
    his miracles, and the rulings he has given,
your children of his servant Israel,
    you descendants of Jacob, his chosen ones.

He is the Lord our God.
    His justice is seen throughout the land.
Remember his covenant forever—
    the commitment he made to a thousand generations,
this is the covenant he made with Abraham
    and the oath he swore to Isaac.
He confirmed it to Jacob as a decree,
    and to the people of Israel as a never-ending covenant:
"I will give you the land of Canaan as your special possession."

He said this when you were few in number,
    a tiny group of strangers in Canaan.
They wandered from nation to nation,
    from one kingdom to another.
Yet he not let anyone oppress them.
    He warned kings on their behalf:
"Do not touch my chosen people,
    and do not hurt my prophets."

Let the whole earth sing to the Lord!
    Each day proclaim the good news that he saves.
Publish his glorious deeds among the nations.
    Tell everyone about the amazing things he does.

Great is the Lord! He is most worthy of praise!
     He is to be feared above all gods.
The gods of other nations are mere idols,
     but the Lord made the heavens!
Honor and majesty surround him;
     strength and joy fill his dwelling.

O nations of the world, recognize the Lord,
     recognize that the Lord is glorious and strong.
Give to the Lord the glory he deserves!
     Bring your offering and come into his presence.
Worship the Lord in all his holy splendor.
     Let all the earth tremble before him.
The world stands firm and cannot be shaken.

Let the heavens be glad, and the earth rejoice!
     Tell all the nations. "The Lord reigns!"
Let the sea and everything in it shout his praise!
     Let the fields and their crops burst out with joy!
Let the trees of the forest rustle with praise,
     for the Lord is coming to judge the earth.

Give thanks to the Lord, for he is good!
     His faithful love endures forever.
Cry out, "Save us, O God for our salvation!
     Gather and rescue us from among the nations,
so we can thank your holy name
     and rejoice and praise you."

Praise the Lord, the God of Israel,
     who lives from everlasting to everlasting!

Then I looked over the situation, I called together the nobles and the rest of the people and said to them. Don't be afraid of the enemy! Remember the Lord, who is great and glorious, and fight for your brothers, your sons, your daughters, your wives, and your homes.

Nehemiah 4:14

Chapter Six

Defensive Warfare
(Weapons of Mass Destruction)

Chapter Six: Defensive Warfare

Defensive warfare is combat battle waged skillfully with powerful weapons of mass destruction to defend financial blessings released for God's children. Weapons of mass destruction are children of God who are fully suited in spiritual armor with the potential to cause great damage to every financial stronghold.

Many believers become victims to financial strongholds and find themselves dreading bill collectors calling their homes, jobs, friends or businesses.

Financial enemies often disguise themselves as a friend in the beginning to the financially illiterate with distractions regarding the truth about loan or business contracts. In addition, financial enemies often use this technique as a way to release nasty letters injected with fear, sent to intimidate their victims into giving up everything they own at a later date.

Financial enemies usually have no compassion when it comes to a job loss or mercy when your child is in the hospital. Defensive warfare simply means the attack from the enemy has caught you off guard. The enemy has entered your home, checks are bouncing, bank fees are rising and you have two choices, defend yourself or die. You are beyond a state of emergency. This is time to remember who you are in Christ and fight back with all you've got!

The primary goal of war is to gain an advantage. It is self-defeating for an individual to pretend that he or she is in control of their finances with debt so high that it would take four generations to fight. You must not be afraid of financial strongholds. You must prepare and arm yourself with enough fire power to destroy selected financial enemies and other targets without delay.

Fighting a defensive financial war means that it's time for you to take responsibility so as to become financially stable. Winning this war means taking strategic action immediately by putting on the whole armor of God. You are not powerless. Therefore, learn how to wage war successfully against every pickpocket in the spirit and earth realm.

God's children must be alert to financial invasions. Defend your territory by refusing "no money down" deals with a thirty or more year payment plan. Save ahead for the things you desire. Stop all financial attacks and invasions immediately!

Put on all of God's armor so that you will be able to stand firm against all strategies of the devil. **Ephesians 6:11**

It should be mandatory for every church or institution to implement a financial education sector to teach their partners or members about basic budgeting skills, employment readiness and how to start their own business. God's children must fight for their brothers and sisters who are trapped in their mind about their financial destination.

It is no longer acceptable for teachers, leaders, pastors and priests to accept dues and tithes without providing basic financial resources and training for their members. Those days are over! God command these wolves in sheep clothing to step down, pull back, and make room for his children who are dressed in full armor with the ability to use their spiritual weapons correctly.

Therefore, put on every piece of God's armor so that you will be able to resist the enemy in the time of evil. Then after the battle you will still be standing firm.
Ephesians 6:13

Defense Weapon #1: Financial Belt (Truth)

Wearing your financial belt is the first defensive weapon needed to activate in order to secure financial territory. A financial belt acts as a balancer during a defensive attack and is the foundation for your full armor. Fighters must be grounded in the absolute truth of financial scriptures.

Being grounded with financial scriptures prepares fighters to fight back with power when an attack occurs. Understanding the truth about financial scriptures will set you free from the devil's lies concerning your financial destination.

The truth about your current financial situation is a result of practicing self-defeating behaviors that have caused past and present financial advancement towards wealth or poverty. It is not God's fault if you refused to use financial scriptures daily. It is not the devil's fault if you willingly withhold the tithe.

Fighters must take full responsibility for personal financial battles. Those who think lack, produce lack. Those who think riches produce riches. It is no one else's fault when you run up a $100,000 debt on a $40, 000 a year salary.

Thoughts of greed and envy produce high debt. Facing the truth about your relationship with money is necessary before you can experience financial freedom. Therefore learn how to stand your ground and fight against the lies that you chose to believe about your ability to create more wealth.

Lying about your financial situation so that you can fit into a group is never worth it. Every lie will one day be exposed. Just by pulling your credit report you can find out immediately where you stand financially. For many, facing your credit report and creating a plan to clear each negative report one at a time will bring immediate light to a financial situation that was once very dark.

Wearing a financial belt during an attack prepares God's children to keep focus on the mission of subduing all situations. A financial belt is an effective defensive weapon that once activated will bring guidance and insight as to how to defend your financial territory with the Holy Spirit.

Some Questions to Face Before and During a Financial Attack Include:
1. What is your current net worth?
2. How much is your total debt?
3. What is your credit score?
4. Do you lie about how much you really make?
5. Do you provide a special offering annually for your financial mentor?
6. Are you welcoming others with the same dysfunction of being an emotional spender with little to no investments?

Stand your ground, putting on the belt of truth and the body armor of God's righteousness. **Ephesians 6:14**

Defense Weapon #2: Financial Breastplate (Justice)

Putting on your financial breastplate is a defense weapon with enough fire power to cover you with God's righteousness; a necessary weapon to protect you against an attack. Your financial breastplate can only be activated by respecting and following the ways of God.

Following God's way is your path to safety during a financial war, there is no success without it. Your financial breastplate must also be tightly and safely attached to your financial belt.

Children of God must use the righteousness of God to respond to creditors properly. It will open up doors of financial favor with mortgage companies, divorce courts and banking institutions with foreclosure listings that has your name on it.

Do not begin your day without putting on your breastplate. Cover all financial bases by reviewing your checking account balance daily or weekly. Review your savings and investments accounts with excitement.

For those who do not have a savings or investment account, research banks and institutions to see who will give the highest return for borrowing your money. Investigate credit unions and online savings banks such as State Farm and ING. Increase your knowledge base about the banking system and use it to make better financial decisions.

Wearing your breastplate positions you to eliminate over spending and produce fewer financial mistakes. Overspending is a byproduct of fear. The fear of not having enough; thinking in limitation, creates overspending. Your breastplate is designed to counterattack these limited thoughts. There are unlimited riches available to all God's children. Embrace this idea and win your financial war.

Create a financial plan to pay bills on time before your next pay period. Your financial plans should consist of a short-term (within twelve months), intermediate (within one-three years), and long-term (three-five years) goals. Meet with your financial mentor ahead of time to plan your goals and rewards. Do not wait until payday to begin planning. This is lack of faith. Act **NOW!**

Having faith and believing God has called you to prosper is necessary for survival in this financial war. This is not the time to procrastinate when paying off your debt. Look for new and exciting ways to share your wealth and receive God's righteousness by creating a ten-year financial plan.

It is amazing what God will do for those who obey his commands. Put God to the test. Develop a charitable attitude. This is the time to know who you are in Christ. You are no longer shadow boxing. It's time to win.

Stay alert! Watch out for your great enemy, the devil. He prowls around like a roaring lion, looking for someone to devour. Stand firm against him, and be strong in your faith. Remember that your Christian brothers and sisters all over the world are going through the same kind of suffering you are. **1 Peter 5:8,9**

Defense Weapon #3: Financial Shoes (Peace)

Financial shoes are defense weapons to be worn at all times. The gospel of peace (shoes) is one of the greatest resources you will need in order to step on the neck of every financial enemy that dares to launch an attack at you.

Wearing your shoes during battle increases your ability for endurance by connecting you to God's unlimited support and guidance. The gospel of peace will position you to stay calm and confident during financial storms. Refusing to wear your financial shoes during battle only produce mental chaos and prolong the battles in your mind.

According to Psalm 34:19, many are the afflictions of the righteous.

At all times learn to be content with your current situation. Your shoes will fail to activate if you are constantly complaining about the lack of money and opportunities available. God did not say you would not have financial problems. Nor did he say you would be at peace if you went to church.

If you do not have enough money presently, you should activate your defensive weapons and tie the laces on your financial shoes and begin to walk faster by speaking financial scriptures directly to your bank books, job, bills and savings accounts out loud.

Your shoes should be worn to organize bills and to communicate with creditors when scheduling payment plans. Not knowing how much you owe, or the penalty for not paying on time is an action of laying down your arms. This kind of action will not produce peace during a battle.

The ultimate goal in wearing your financial shoes is to experience peace with all financial transaction. Put savings and investment accounts under surveillance and keep track of fees and interest earned on all accounts.

God is Lord of every financial battle that you will ever fight. God is in complete control of every situation. Financial distress will only occur when you want something before provisions are released. Distress with debt is a sign of greed.

There is no peace with debt. You must learn to seek God for the ultimate economic plan for each item you desire before purchasing. Being lazy in writing out a savings plan before your next purchase will produce debt in your future.

Debt is not connected to God. When Jesus died on the cross he released peace to your financial situation. God purchased his children free and clear with the blood of Jesus Christ. Wear your shoes by not rushing or hurrying to accomplish a financial goal before God releases his resources to you.

For shoes, put on the peace that comes from the Good News so that you will be fully prepared. **Ephesians 6:15**

Defense Weapon #4: Financial Shield (Faith)

Financial success belongs to all of God's children. Take action today by increasing your faith level. Your financial shield is a strategic defense weapon that should be used as a weapon against negative thoughts about your financial situation. Trust God to bring the right people into your life. Trust God with every decision until you gain financial victory.

Doubt equals debt and faith equals wealth. Have faith in your ability to become a strong financial warrior. Develop habits that support your debt free thinking by reading and listening to this book over and over until it makes sense to you. Increased faith comes through hearing the word of God. Listen attentively, and defend your inheritance with confidence.

Begin and end each day knowing your wealth is increasing. Faith cannot exist with negative thoughts. Not wearing your shield allows financial enemies to take up residence in your mind, and eventually your wallet.

Wearing your financial shield will always make room for greatness to enter your life. Doors that were once closed will now be wide open. Creditors will make arrangements you never thought possible because of your increased faithfulness. There will be no failures when your financial shield is safely attached to your belt.

Have faith in your ability to create more income. Refuse to repeat the cycle of poverty. You are no longer the working poor. You are a creative and powerful spiritual weapon with unlimited talents and abilities. You will win!

You already possess great and exciting ideas with the ability to bring millions of dollars to your home. Your ability to attract synergistic and wealthy partnerships is all at your finger tips. You are not alone. The creator of heaven and earth is always with you, preparing you to win.

Begin your day with a financial map that clearly lists your goals for each day. Use your map to travel safely to your inheritance. Do not turn right or left. Stay directly on the path mapped out. You will have success every time you activate your defense weapons skillfully.

Do not agree to travel to an unscheduled financial destination. Do not settle for a $30,000 annual salary if it's your heart desire to earn $200,000 annually and debt free. Use your financial shield as a travel guide to your ultimate destination. Financial victory belongs to you and your household all the time!

It is the will of God for all his children to prosper and be in good health.

"You don't have enough faith," Jesus told them. "I tell you the truth, if you had faith even as small as a mustard seed, you could say to this mountain, 'Move from here to there,' and it would move. Nothing would be impossible." **Matthew 17:20**

Just because you cannot see your financial victory does not mean it's not there. Supernatural increase is revealed only to those who believe before seeing.

Activating your financial shield is needed especially when darkness surrounds your finances. Lack of faith limits your ability to see what God is doing on your behalf. God has heard every prayer you cried or whispered to him. God is very much concerned about your financial situation. He cares about your ability to create great wealth and success. Wearing your financial shield commands light to shine on all financial darkness.

You should lend your ears closely to God's truth about financial increase. Show no mercy to your financial strongholds and strap on your shield tightly. Wearing your financial shield is a deliberate attempt to put on the character of God whose ways you may not understand.

When financial fear is cultivated it produces low paying jobs, overspending, and children who produce the same as their parents. Wearing your financial shield is achieving mastery at every level; a debt free home, children who respect money and an income level that sees no limit.

Your present financial battles can sometimes limit your actions and blind your vision about your destiny. However, this defensive weapon often transforms itself into a spiritual radar with the capability to see through all financial fogginess. Nothing goes undetected, when you wear your financial shield. Every enemy is exposed ahead of time. Praise the Lord!

Courage to call creditors when you are behind on bills is a character of one who believes in financial victory. Courage to be creative and inventive during war is an attribute of fighters who are not afraid to activate and use their defensive weapons until every battle is won. Financial despair, anxiety and laziness are characteristics of those who refuse to be financially responsible.

Fighters who wear their shield have faith. Therefore, no explanation is necessary during a financial crisis. These individuals remain steadfast and listen well. Listening to mentors who teach the Word of God will help to increase your faith. However, those who refuse to listen to what God have to say about achieving financial independence will suffer greatly.

*But let us who live in the light be clearheaded, protected by the armor of faith and love, and wearing as our helmet the confidence of our salvation. **1 Thessalonians 5:8***

__Defense Weapon #5A: Financial Helmet (Salvation)__

God's love for his children is infinite. The defensive weapon of salvation is available to all. By putting on your financial helmet you are inviting Christ into your daily decisions and increasing your ability to succeed with all financial goals.

God's salvation allows direct access to his infinite knowledge and wisdom. Receiving salvation often releases wisdom that shows step by step how to get out of debt and how to secure unlimited financial increase. Because God is omniscient, he will reveal several financial destinations, declaring the end from the beginning. This is a gift from the Lord; you cannot buy it.

__Questions to Ask Yourself Before Putting on Your Helmet__:
1. Do I believe that Jesus Christ died for my sins?
2. Can God show me a way out of my financial crisis?
3. Am I tired of paying my bills late?
4. Do I get frustrated when I think about money?
5. Is God available 24/7 to hear my request?
6. Am I ready to receive Christ as my Lord?

If you answered "yes" to all the questions above, you are now ready to put on your helmet. The power of salvation allows God to create multimillionaires and unlimited wealth increased through his children. Nothing is too mighty for God to do in your life when you put him first. Whatever you ask in Jesus Name not doubting, will be granted.

Seek the Kingdom of God first and everything you desire will happen for you. God is not millions of miles away during a financial crisis. God is omnipresent. He's at your job. He's with you when you pay your bills. He's also with you when you become frustrated with money. God is always beside you, waiting for you to invite him into your life. Welcome God's salvation and receive financial stability today.

In addition, God is holy. A holy God will not allow you to use his money for lustful pleasures and then bless you with inner peace. God will not reward you for being unkind to the poor. You will reap what you sow!

If you turn your back on family members who are in need, God will turn his back on your needs. If you bless others with your financial increase, God will continue to bless you with riches and wealth. God's holiness covers those who receive him as Lord. Once you invite God into your life, being a better steward with his money becomes automatic. The salvation of God will make you very rich without sorrow.

And they were shouting with a mighty shout, "Salvation comes from our God who sits on the Throne and from the Lamb!" ***Revelation 7:10***

God's mercy and compassion for you will never fail. When you do not pay your tithes, he shows mercy. When you do not prepare ahead of time for retirement or for your children's college education, he shows compassion. God's salvation will show you a way out of all financial troubles. He will never leave you or forsake you. God is patiently waiting for you to put on your financial helmet so that he can display himself victoriously through you.

No power on earth can defeat God's economic plan for those who wear their financial helmet. It is impossible to stand against a child of God who is grateful for salvation. God's economic plan for you will not return void. You will not return void to God because of the power that comes with receiving salvation.

God's purpose for you to be the head and not the tail will be established in the earth without delay. There are no failures with God's economic plan. Continuously look to God for new and exciting ideas. Activate words of increase and multiplication using your voice to set the atmosphere right each day. Wear your financial helmet during all times and seasons boldly.

Christ died and rose from the dead so that you might have everlasting financial increase and a high quality of life. God's children are lenders, not borrowers. You already have financial victory against every stronghold that tries to keep you in bondage. Do not take a day off in activating this defensive weapon.

God is unchangeable and you are precious to him. Therefore, your financial state is constantly on God's mind. Jehovah Nissi wants you to experience abundance. There are millions of projects and ideas waiting for you to invest in. Prepare for victory!

* How can you invest without money?
* How can God's glory be seen if you are unemployed?
* How can family members come to Christ if they hear your constant complain about lack of money?
* Why would your neighbors come to Christ if you are always borrowing from them?

God's children never beg, and they will never be abandoned. The Gospel is good news for all. God's financial scriptures are priceless. Scriptures work if you use them. As a child of the King; you must not ignore the **urgency** in being released from all financial strongholds. You are not the enemies' footstool. You were bought with a very high price. God's love for you is supreme above all.

Christ is your Savior. There is no other. Seek financial wisdom by allowing Christ's confidence and boldness to fill your mind with thoughts that produce unlimited success daily. Allow your Savior to radiate financial power and strength through every project and idea that comes through you. God is waiting for you to make the decision; receive salvation now. Invite Christ into your life today. Put on your financial helmet and be free to live abundantly wealthy.

He alone is my rock and my salvation, my fortress where I will never be shaken.

Psalm 62:2

Defense Weapon #5B: Financial Sword (Word of God)

The Word of God is alive. Using your sword during an attack is a combat answer to every financial stronghold. No financial distress can survive when you use your financial sword. A financial attack is non-existent in the presence of a warrior who knows how to use their sword skillfully.

*The Word gave life to everything that was created, and his life brought light to everyone. **John 1:4***

The Word of God is Christ in full armor. You cannot separate Christ from your financial experiences. It is Christ in full armor that goes before you and grants financial favor with creditors and your boss.

It is Christ through his Spirit who exposes those who try to deceive and mislead you financially. The financial sword can be a powerful and explosive weapon in the hands of those who love and obey God.

The more you are exposed to financial scriptures, the more the Spirit can use this mighty financial sword during an attack. Lack of financial scriptures means you are not prepared and cannot activate the financial sword to work on your behalf. Financial scriptures are bullets loaded into the heart ahead of time so that when an attack occurs all you need to do is fire-speak the Word. **Firing a gun without bullets is insane!**

There is no defense without using your financial sword. During a financial attack it is important to know how to defend yourself properly. Use your financial sword to speak life to your debts daily and back the enemy off your property and possessions. Give yourself permission to leave financial hell immediately.

Saturate your eyes and ears gate with financial scriptures daily. Keep your financial sword in your hands. Do not store your bible on the book shelve until the next time you go to church. It will be too late. Spend time reading, listening and searching the bible daily for every financial bullet that you can find. This action is necessary to gain ground.

Reflect upon past financial whopping and scars as motivation to learn how to use your financial sword with purpose.

The center of your life is Jesus Christ. The Word of God is the key to every battle; heed and obey. Nothing is hidden from God. Do not reject the power that comes from using your financial sword fearlessly.

*For the word of God is alive and powerful. It is sharper than the sharpest two-edged sword, cutting between soul and spirit, between joint and marrow. It exposes our innermost thoughts and desires. Nothing in all creation is hidden from God. Everything is naked and exposed before his eyes, and he is the one to whom we are accountable. **Hebrews 4:12,13***

Do not enter a financial battle field half-dressed. Do not speak with a bill collector without your financial sword. This war is hungry for casualties. Put God's financial scriptures in your heart everyday.

Do not underestimate creditor's ability to repossess your cars, home or furniture. Raise above all these petty battles and prepare to fight greater battles like defending your billion dollar dreams or establishing an on-site banking system in every church across the nation.

Those who neglect to use their financial sword are in disobedience to the Will of God. God set you on planet earth and command that you multiply, subdue, replenish, dominate, and bear fruit. It is impossible to accomplish such an assignment without the use of your financial sword.

You are not a victim to strongholds. You are God's sheep. You lack nothing. If you are without work, improve your skills and actively seek to be productive. If you are not increasing your finances annually, seek out new opportunities or partnerships. Refusing to use your financial sword daily is an excuse for laziness and overspending. Financial errors are results of continuous refusal to use your sword.

1. Are you late more than once with paying your bills?
2. Do you allow late fees to double or sometimes triple?
3. Do you bounce your tithes?
4. Are you a fan of "Check Cashing" venues?
5. Do you still think you know everything about financial strongholds?

God's children must use their financial sword wisely and take the battle sometimes to the enemy by paying bills three, sometimes six months ahead. This simple act strips the enemy of their own armor leaving them defenseless. There will be no late fees or payments to collect for a while, hence you have gained territory. Your next step is to use the same financial strategy over and over until financial freedom is evident not only in your life, but in the lives of everyone God assigns to you.

Financial victory will come every time you use your sword with confidence. To be more than a conqueror with your finances, you must:

1. Surrender all false beliefs about your financial situation to God.
2. Kill all desires for the lust of the flesh.
3. Believe that you already have financial victory.
4. Have faith in God (not man) with every financial battle.
5. Refuse to live with limitations.
6. Constantly secure financial increase.
7. Love God by giving generously to others.

Trust only in the Lord. Do not follow your own ideas and understanding. You were created for such a time as this. Defend your financial territories with power!

The Lord merely spoke, and the heavens were created. He breathed the word, and all the stars were born. **Psalm 33:6**

Defense Weapon #6: Financial Prayer (Thanking God)

The perfect financial prayer you can express to God is gratefulness. There is no need to pray for financial increase over and over again. God has already released all the wealth and riches for each of his children before the foundation of the earth. All financial gates, portals and doors are wide open. There is nothing new for God to create.

Everything you need in order to become productive is already here on planet earth. Take the time to express gratefulness while on the job or during a business transaction. Open your refrigerator and pantry with a grateful heart to the Lord God Almighty who has blessed your family day after day. The same God that took care of you yesterday is the same God who will take care of you again today.

Look at your husband, wife and children giving God thanks for their successes. Using your financial prayers as a weapon will always draw God's wisdom, wealth and riches closer to you, your family, your friends and your community.

Do not pray for an easier job or a richer spouse. Pray to be an individual that brings constant increase to every job opportunity and relationship. Pray that God will impregnate you with a skill that is equal to the unlimited ability God has already supplied to you. Then, by using your financial prayers as a weapon your production level will reach a standard that brings amazing glory to God.

Pray in the spirit for a debt free home and pray with love. Pray with compassion for your creditors. Thank God for his forgiveness with your irresponsibility with the income he gave you. Give God thanks for releasing forgiveness to the creditors who called your job and spoke to co-workers about your financial situation.

Thank God for blessing your ex-spouse who recently filed a petition with the courts to garnish your check. Pray in obedience when paying your tithes to the Heavenly Father. Pray with confidence about every financial situation. Pray believing that you already have the answer from God. Pray with a grateful heart. In other words, use your financial prayers as a weapon to pray a prayer that Jesus himself would pray.

Work daily as if you were already a millionaire. Give generously as if you had an abundance of wealth. Pay your bills as if you were financially responsible. Use your defensive weapons boldly and pray as if today was your best and blessed day.

The eyes of the Lord watch over those who do right, and his ears are open to their prayers. But the Lord turns his face against those who do evil. **1 Peter 3:12**

Many pray as if God were a drug dealer and some pray only when they are in financial trouble. Then, once God fixes the situation, praying is no longer the priority. The fix was good until the next time.

Wishing to be rich and debt free will never become a substitute for using your defensive weapons. Using your financial prayers as a weapon involves thought and action. God has unlimited ideas capable of producing financial increase for you. God is patiently waiting to hear his favorite words from you "**Thank you Lord**".

Learn to cherish your Holy relationship between you and God. If you are unemployed, in debt, and unhappy, fast and pray. If you are wealthy, debt free, and very happy, fast and pray. There is no quick fix to your financial situation. Thanking God during a trial or in times of increase is important. Your relationship with God is more than a quickie; it is eternal.

Ask your Heavenly Father to provide your financial needs. The bible says "we receive not, because we do not ask". Financial prayers can be used to shield your soul and is a special offering to God. It is also a discouragement to all your bill collectors. Using financial prayers makes you strong.

It is impossible to live one way and pray another. Therefore learn to alter your life by using financial prayers as a weapon to move closer to God. Do not overspend and then ask God for increase. Do not rob God of the tithes and get mad at the church for not paying your bills. Become financially responsible and understand that you cannot serve two masters.

Those who do not believe that God can fix their financial situations constantly complain about increased price on everything, which keeps them in bondage. Those who accept God's economic principles pray, giving thanks daily while those with unbelief do not pray at all.

A child of God who neglects to pay their bills within a timely manner makes their financial enemy smile. When a child of God stops studying the bible, the devil gets excited. However, when a child of God stops using their financial prayers as a weapon daily, the devil throws a party and shouts "They fell for my trick, again!"

Always acknowledge that God is your heavenly Father who takes care of all your needs. Enter his presence with praise, respect and humility. God is not your genie. He is the one true God who created all things in the universe for his glory. God loves you and seeks to express himself in a great and mighty way through you.

Pray for God's economic will to be done in your life, so that the glory he receives in heaven is also the glory received through you on earth. Remember, you are created to serve God, not your limited imagination.

*Never stop praying. **1 Thessalonians 5:17***

Defense Weapon #7: Financial Testimony (Victory)

A financial testimony is a defensive weapon that provides a form of evidence supporting the fact that you are truly a child of the Most High. God's children are not bastards. Therefore, there should be enough physical evidence for others to see very clearly that the Spirit of the living God exists and rules in your life.

Some evidence may include a debt free home, secured investments, a retirement plan, lending to the community and being generous in giving. Becoming a financial testimony for the body of Christ is a weapon that brings immediate evidence through the blood of the lamb.

Becoming a financial testimony to your family, your friends and your community means that you are an expert witness to the glory of God. There will be no call for speculation. You must be clearly identified by the financial fruits you bear for the body of Christ, not by hearsay. A financial testimony is a defensive weapon that is considered to be a precious commodity, especially during the course of becoming an expert witness for the Lord.

The best evidence always rules. A warrior with a financial testimony does not have low self-esteem. There is no lack of financial foundation; so with great confidence and humility these warriors allow others to experience the truth about Christ through godly relationships. Becoming a financial testimony is another great form of evidence you must develop so as to win this war victoriously.

There is always an obligation to defend your savings and investments. Therefore, a burden of proof is issued to children of the Most High God to prove beyond a reasonable doubt that common sense and success belongs to them. Practice clear and convincing principles that follow all economic plans designed by God.

Financial testimonies in the form of opinions or inferences are often limited and are irrelevant during a financial war. God is not interested in excuses about why you are in debt. God wants to know "what have you done with the finances to glorify him?" Is there enough evidence beyond a reasonable doubt that God's money was used effectively to produce increase of one, two, three or more percent, or was it used to sponsor activities created to support the lust of your flesh?

Children of God, who live in mortgaged homes, entertain credit cards like a form of income and drive expensive cars attached to outrageous loans and interest rates have committed a serious crime in the body of Christ. This is perjury. Your credit report gives proof. Become free in Christ!

In that wonderful day you will sing: "Thank the Lord! Praise his name! Tell the nations what he has done. Let them know how mighty he is! **Isaiah 12:4**

There is plenty of evidence in the bible to support the fact that God wants his children blessed. God wants you to prosper and live a long life. God wants you to be a **lender and generous giver**, not an over spender.

Your financial testimony must reflect God's glory at all times. Obedience to God is establishing a strategic savings plan which is necessary for financial advancement. Operating at this level leaves no room for procrastinators. Re-read chapter one and learn how to conquer laziness and move on to developing a financial victory mentality.

There is probable cause to support the fact that many of God's children do produce a relatively low standard of proof in regards to their financial testimony. These are individuals who may pay their tithes, pay their bills on time, but do not have enough to help others who are in need.

Low standard producing Christians have some form of evidence, but not enough to bring a full conviction. Becoming a financial testimony should leave no doubt with your families, your friends and your community that you are a powerful and mighty weapon of mass destruction against financial strongholds.

Claiming victory concludes that the Lord is your Shepherd. Therefore you lack nothing and the people assigned to your life lack nothing. There are many needs to be met in your family and your community. The numbers are climbing higher, year after year, for those who are homeless and left for dead.

How can you say you are a child of God with so many unmet financial needs in your community? Why do you tolerate debt and unemployment as a way to glorify God? Where in the bible does it declare that God's children are not cared for? What evil imagination did you allow to enter your mind about your possibilities of becoming prosperous? It's time to stop accepting poverty as a way of life.

You are assigned as a financial underwriter to meet the needs of the community you live in. The income you receive must be used responsibly to care for your needs and the needs of others. Do not spend 100% of your income on yourself. This negative act will activate financial failure for you, your family, and, anyone connected to you.

Reverse all financial curses in your home today by supporting your local food bank or begin a clothing drive for those looking for jobs. Many of God's children are assigned in the community to teach. Others are assigned to empower and motivate the uneducated and those who battle thoughts of lack. The spiritual gifts God gave you will make room for you. Testify loudly through your actions that Jesus Christ is Lord!

And they have defeated him by the blood of the Lamb and by their testimony.
Revelation 12:11

Sample Declaration of Financial War against Strongholds

Name of Stronghold: #1 Credit Card Company

Amount of the Attack: $3000

Goal: To pay in full by July 30th

Scripture: *So I run with purpose in every step. I am not just shadowboxing.*
                                            1 Corinthians 9:26

Financial Strategy:
1. Listen to the bible one hour at the beginning of each day.
2. Fast one day weekly until victory is achieved against #1 Credit Card Company.
3. Ask God for increase faith to win battle against #1 Credit Card Company.
4. Confess financial scripture daily.
5. Cut back on emotional spending and increase giving to others.
6. Spend one minute daily meditating on strategies for achieving complete victory.
7. Make monthly payments on time to #1 Credit Card Company.
8. Make weekly or monthly extra payments until mission is accomplished.
9. Celebrate success of winning financial battle against #1 Credit Card Company.
10. Prepare to advance financially by writing out a declaration of financial war for each stronghold.

Financial Prayer: Father God, thank you for giving me a speedy victory in paying #1 Credit Card Company $3000 before July 30th. There is none like you Lord. Amen!

Evaluation:
- Made payments on time.
- Saved coffee money and applied to credit card bill as extra weekly payments.
- Paid credit card bill ahead of schedule (Thank you Jesus!)

Chapter Six: Defensive Warfare Summary

Defense Weapon #1 Financial Belt (Truth)
Wear financial belt as a balancer to face the truth regarding the amount of personal debt that needs your attention during a defensive attack.

Defense Weapon #2 Financial Breastplate (Justice)
Put on the financial breastplate for protection before responding to creditors during a defensive attack.

Defense Weapon #3 Financial Shoes (Peace)
Wear financial shoes at all times to organize and pay bills.

Defense Weapon #4 Financial Shield (Faith)
Attach your financial shield safely to belt until habits that support a debt free thinking are developed.

Defense Weapon #5A Financial Helmet (Salvation)
Wear financial helmet to experience infinite financial increase. Do not begin your day without wearing your helmet.

Defense Weapon #5B Financial Sword (Word of God)
The financial sword is a powerful and mighty defensive weapon in the hands of those who love and obey God.

Defense Weapon #6 Financial Prayer (Thankfulness)
Use your financial prayers to deal with creditors and lenders who have become financial strongholds.

Defense Weapon #7 Financial Testimony (Victory)
Become a financial testimony that clearly displays God's glory without doubt.

Chapter Six: Voice Activated Financial Confessions

Greater is he that is in me than he that is in the world.

I boldly walk in different directions knowing that God is getting ready to give it to me.

I am a financial testimony for the Lord.

No weapons formed against my economic situation will prosper.

I am strategically prepared for all financial battles.

My plans and decisions reflect God's plans for my life.

I am a powerful financial authority on the earth.

I demand all good things to come to me right now.

My financial plans are blessed by the Lord.

I wear my financial shoes proudly.

God's faithful words are eternal, therefore I celebrate victory daily.

If God is with me; who can be against me?

Those who help others are blessed. I help others therefore I am blessed.

Thank you Lord for teaching me, how to be a powerful weapon of mass destruction.

God is in charge of my financial plans so I will prosper and have great success.

My steadfastness reflects God's favor in my life.

I represent God with power.

God has fulfilled the promises he made to me.

I meditate on God's word day and night to confirm my success.

The Lord is good to those who depend and search for him. Therefore, I search for him ceaselessly.

Financial Warfare Deliverance Song
Exodus 15:1-18

I will sing to the Lord,
For he has triumphed gloriously;
He has hurled both horse and rider into the sea.

The Lord is my strength and my song;
He has given me victory.
This is my God, and I will praise him-
My father's God, and I will exalt him!

The Lord is a warrior; Yahweh* is his name!
Pharaoh's chariots and army
He has hurled into the sea.
The deep waters gushed over them;
They sank to the bottom like a stone.

Your right hand, O Lord,
Is glorious in power.
Your right hand, O Lord,
Smashes the enemy.
In the greatness of your majesty,
You overthrow those who rise against you.
You unleash your blazing fury;
It consumes them like straw.
At the blast of your breath,
The waters piled up!
The surging waters stood straight like a wall;
In the heart of the sea the deep waters became hard.

The enemy boasted, "I will chase them
And catch up with them.
I will plunder them and consume them.
I will flash my sword;
My powerful hand will destroy them.'
But you blew with your breath,
And the sea covered them.
They sank like lead in the mighty waters.

Who is like you among the gods, O Lord-
Glorious in holiness, awesome in splendor,
Performing great wonders?
You raised your right hand,
And the earth swallowed our enemies.

With your unfailing love you lead
The people you have redeemed.
In your might, you guide them
To your sacred home.
The peoples hear and tremble;
Anguish grips those who live in Philistia.
The leaders of Edom are terrified;
The nobles of Moab tremble.
All who live in Canaan melt away;
Terror and dread fall upon them.
The power of your arm
Makes them lifeless as stone
Until your people pass by, O Lord,
Until the people you purchased pass by.
You will bring them in and plant them on your own
Mountain—the place, O Lord, reserved for your own dwelling.
The Sanctuary, O Lord, that your hands have established.
The Lord will reign forever and ever!

We are humans, but we don't wage war as humans do. We use God's mighty weapons not worldly weapons, to knock down the strongholds of human reasoning and to destroy false arguments.

2 Corinthians 10:3,4

Chapter Seven

Spiritual Weaponry
(Smart Ammo)

Chapter Seven: Spiritual Weaponry for Financial War

Understanding the correct use of spiritual weaponry for financial warfare commands unlimited wealth and riches to the user. Spiritual weaponry (smart ammo) provides God's children with effective tools that can be used to stop financial attacks during all times and seasons. This war must not be fought using carnal weapons.

Spiritual weaponry is to be used as a powerful aid to protect you from being killed in this financial war. You cannot survive this war without using God's spiritual weapons to defend and protect yourself successfully.

Embracing God's spiritual weapons will do the following:
  1. Detect a financial attack ahead of time
  2. Reveal intelligent insight about financial predators
  3. Assign well armed Angels to protect all financial increase
  4. Identify potential financial risk and expose them
  5. Safe guard all savings and investment accounts

The basic task your spiritual weapons will perform has not changed since the resurrection of Jesus Christ. If you have been born again by the power of the Holy Spirit, you are eligible to receive the things of the Spirit of God. If you have not accepted Jesus Christ into your life, this would be a good time to do so. Read the invitation prayer for unbelievers at the end of this chapter for assistance.

When you display irresponsible behavior that mirrors the lust of the flesh as discussed in Chapter four and five; it simply means you do not know how to use your spiritual weaponry.

Your spiritual weaponry should be used effectively to fight creditors who use the working poor to build large and successful businesses. Due to limited financial education, creditors repeatedly lend large sums of money with very high revolving interest rates, hoping to produce life time debtors.

Preparing yourself properly with spiritual weapons will stop creditors immediately from taking advantage of your lack of financial wisdom.

Implementing spiritual weapons will reflect back to you the successful culture of heaven; an intense and great desire that pleases God. You do not need another loan. Develop a strong economic plan using God's spiritual weapons as a major tool in winning this war.

The sinful nature wants to do evil, which is just the opposite of what the Spirit wants. And the Spirit gives us desires that are the opposite of what the sinful nature desires.
Galatians 5 verse 17

A clear sign that one is a carrier of God's spiritual weapon can be seen in the physical manifestation of the fruit of the spirit. A display of the fruit of the spirit means no attack of the enemy will ever get through. You might get hit, but it will never harm you.

From the beginning of each day to the end of each night you must be ready to use the fruit of the spirit as a weapon against every financial stronghold. Being armed with the fruit of the spirit will protect you from fulfilling the lust of the flesh.

God's spiritual weaponry will position you to be like a tree planted by the rivers of water that prospers and bears good fruit in all seasons.

The fruit of the spirit is given to all believers. God's spiritual weaponry is easily accessible for those who live by the spirit; however it can bring great distress for those who try to use it while living in the flesh. Inappropriate use brings death!

To live without all nine fruit of the spirit is to be completely dead to the great harvest that it brings in abundance. Financial freedom is a choice and starts when you use the fruit of the spirit as a weapon.

The excitement and happiness that comes with using God's weaponry cannot be explained. However, it can be experienced by all. Take my word for it! There is no feeling on earth to match the endless bliss that enters the life of one who uses God's weaponry with purpose. The power to call your bills paid and see it manifested comes only from God. To experience the move of the spirit on your behalf, releases an amazing feeling that cannot be duplicated elsewhere. The power to command financial increase wherever you go is a freedom that so many crave; yet only few experience.

God takes great pleasure in sharing this weapon with you. Make an effort to reach for it before it's too late. Don't wait until you lose your children or your job. Learn the economic principles in this book and re-read it until your subconscious mind accepts that you are victorious with all financial transactions. Cover yourself with the fruit of the spirit and watch miracles happen in your life.

The nine fruit of the spirit (smart ammo) include the following:
1. Love
2. Joy
3. Peace
4. Patience
5. Kindness
6. Self-Control
7. Goodness
8. Faithfulness
9. Meekness

SMART AMMO #1: LOVE

LOVE, is the first and greatest spiritual weapon that must be used at all times during financial warfare. Activating the love of God means your harvest is already here. There are no worries about financial stability. The love of God is a seed that must be planted generously so that the return can generate continuous increase.

What is God's love?

Love never gives up.
Love cares more for others than for self.
Love doesn't want what it doesn't have.
Love doesn't strut,
Doesn't have a swelled head,
Doesn't force itself on others,
Isn't always "me first,"
Doesn't fly off the handle,
Doesn't keep score of the sins of others,
Doesn't revel when others grovel,
Takes pleasure in the flowering of truth,
Puts up with anything,
Trusts God always,
Always looks for the best,
Never looks back,
But keeps going to the end.
1 Corinthians 13: 4-7

The amount of love you plant each day will produce a great harvest tomorrow and in your future. You cannot reap God's love if you did not plant it. Creditors will not have a desire to reveal options for paying your bills without the favor of God. You can experience this powerful weapon only when you obey God.

The power of God's love will constantly bring financial favor into your life; favor that cannot be stopped by anyone. Through the power of God's love operating in your life, the needy and the poor will always be cared for. No lack will be around you.

The financial needs of others will be at the top of your daily prayer list. God has already released super-natural resources to increase your finances where you will not have enough room to stock the overflow from heaven. Possessing the character of God's love will gain access to stable and constant financial power.

God's love will increase your desire to give. Love stimulates the desire of generosity and kindness towards all culture and races. God so loves the world that he gave his son Jesus. God loves you so much that he gave you spiritual weapons, discernment with bills and a way out of adversities even when you have been unfaithful. The list of God's love for you is endless.

You should thrive to make love your highest goal in life. Love feels no burden and is not afraid to be financially responsible. With God's love you can position yourself to receive and give without fear. God's love will allow you to take care of family members without complaining. With God's love, you can go to work with contentment knowing that you are working to please God not man.

Blessings for those who give to anyone being controlled by thoughts of poverty and lack:

Those who oppress the poor insult their Maker, but helping the poor honors him.
Proverbs 14:31

Give generously to the poor, not grudgingly, for the Lord your God will bless you in everything you do. **Deuteronomy 15:10**

O the joys of those who are kind to the poor! The Lord rescues them when they are in trouble. **Psalm 41:1**

If you help the poor, you are lending to the Lord-and he will repay you.
Proverbs 19:17

Blessed are those who are generous, because they feed the poor. **Proverbs 22:9**

If you lend money to any of my people who are in need, do not charge interest as a money lender would. **Exodus 22:25**

But if there are any poor Israelites in your towns when you arrive in the land of the Lord your God is giving you, do not be hard-hearted or tightfisted toward them.
Deuteronomy 15:7

If someone has enough money to live well and sees a brother or sister in need but shows no compassion-how can God's love be in that person? 1John 3:17

Examples how to apply the spiritual weapon of God's love:
1. Be satisfied each day.
2. Know that God's love for you is far greater than what you possess.
3. Give God thanks and praise daily for your ability to create wealth.
4. Put the needs of others at the top of your ministry list.
5. Show God that you love him by tithing.
6. Bless others with your money.
7. Create a surveillance plan for your financial goals.

Three things will last forever-faith, hope, love-and the greatest of these is love.
1 Corinthians 13:13

SMART AMMO #2: JOY

JOY is the ideal spiritual weapon to use for protecting your investments. Operating in joy releases God's strength to increase money, bank accounts, investments and all savings that he has already blessed you with.

Possessing joy produces a Spirit that is always thankful to God for providing daily needs and desires. Adopting joy is a secret weapon that releases financial multiplication.

It is in your joyfulness that you can activate the spirit of multiplication. Once the spirit of multiplication is activated; debts are eliminated, all needs are met, and plenty will be left over to give to others.

The ability to cope with daily financial issues depends upon using your smart ammo's effectively and without delay. Your God is a joyful God. He is a God that gets excited every time you succeed at completing your goals. God receives happiness when you become joyful with your giving and receiving.

God gets excited about your ability to receive his joy. It was at a joyous moment when God revealed his son Jesus, and he is waiting patiently for you to experience the same joy that comes through salvation.

No matter what financial problems you are experiencing, you can have comfort knowing that the joy of the Lord is your strength. The anointing of joy will follow you to your job. The anointing of joy will cover you when you sit to pay your bills. The anointing of joy will also comfort you when you express thoughts of doubt and unbelief towards your current financial situation. Supernatural joy provides strength to everyone who chooses God to be their Lord.

Examples how to apply the spiritual weapon of joy:
1. Believe in God's surplus with your investments.
2. Remove fear from your income resources.
3. Know that the Joy of the Lord is your strength.
4. Ask God to turn your financial pain to joy.
5. Anticipate more blessings from God.
6. Obey God's laws.
7. Get out of debt.

Though the cherry trees don't blossom and the strawberries don't ripen, though the apples are worm-eaten and the wheat fields stunted, though the sheep pens are sheep less and the cattle barns empty, I'm singing joyful praise to God. I am turning cartwheels of joy to my Savior God. Counting on God's Rule to prevail, I take heart and gain strength. I run like a deer. I feel like I'm king of the mountain. **Habakkuk 3:17-19**

SMART AMMO #3: PEACE

PEACE is a mandatory spiritual weapon to use for taking more territory. The power of peace activates direct financial increase to the lives of those who are honest with their finances. The spirit of peace can only enter God's children when they pay their tithes and follow all of God's laws regarding giving back to him what he commanded.

The character of peace must rule in your heart. Condition your heart to work very hard towards achieving peace with creditors. The peace of mind that comes with paying bills on time will only follow you when you operate by the law of peace.

There is a peace that surpasses all understanding and it comes directly from God. Just accept God as head of your life and watch closely at the amazing miracles he will pour out of heaven for you.

It is necessary that you think thoughts of abundance when dealing with your finances. Embracing thoughts of abundance will attract positive results to your wallet. Thinking thoughts of lack or disaster will attract an empty wallet.

Financial peace comes from the true and Living God, Jesus Christ. There is no one else who can give peace. Surrender your bills, submit investments and savings to God, and he will give you the gift of peace to deal with all your increased wealth.

You can preserve perfect peace if you train your mind to stay focused on God's economic plan for your life. God will reveal information about your creditors so that the favor of peace will visit your home. Financial tribulations and anxieties are connected to those who are stingy and do not trust God with their finances. However, a child of God will be of good cheer because God goes ahead of them and secures financial victory on the left and on the right. Nothing is too hard for your God!

Examples how to apply the spiritual weapon of peace:
1. Stay in harmony with your bill collectors.
2. Put God at the head of all your financial decisions.
3. Seek God for financial peace.
4. Establish a retirement account.
5. Let the peace of God rule your life.
6. Help with paying your parents bills.
7. Stop borrowing. God's children; do not beg.

I am leaving you with a gift-peace of mind and heart. And the peace I give is a gift the world cannot give. So don't be troubled or afraid. ***John 14:27***

SMART AMMO #4: PATIENCE

PATIENCE is an effective spiritual weapon to use for protecting your assets. The Spirit of patience is persistent and never gives up. No matter how many mistakes are made financially, patience will be there to guide you towards recovery.

When you accept Jesus Christ as Lord of your life, and walk closely with God, you will begin to receive and experience the gift of eternal patience.

Eternal patience is the ability to endure until victory has come. Condition yourself to fight until victory is declared for every financial battle. There is no other way! Each financial battle builds endurance and is designed to lead you closer to God.

The act of overcoming and winning each financial battle will develop more endurance for a race that has already been won by Jesus Christ when he overcame the world. Developing patience brings a successful ending to all financial struggles.

Patience with your finances is needed especially when there is not enough money to cover the bills, groceries or tithes at the beginning of each month. It is through having patience, that storehouses of blessings will be released for you.

Strength and confidence shows up through patience with daily financial transactions. Whenever your finances get low, give thanks and rejoice because God is in control and will step in at just the right time, not your time.

Allowing the Holy Spirit to lead your life will get you out of debt. Remain firm with steadfast conviction that obedience to God is far greater than losing your mind to a financial stronghold. The attribute of patience works well especially during financial conflicts.

Patience is your key to unlocking wealth and riches. Acquire this powerful smart ammo and use it to open all the financial doors that were once closed to you.

Examples how to apply the spiritual weapon of patience:
1. Develop a long-term savings plan.
2. Practice the art of patience daily.
3. Take your time when making financial decisions.
4. Refuse to be lazy with completing a monthly budget.
5. Persevere with learning godly ways to become financially responsible.
6. Wait until retirement before cashing in your 401K.
7. Practice the philosophy of seed time and harvest.

We can rejoice, too, when we run into problems and trials, for we know that they help us develop endurance. **Romans 5:3**

SMART AMMO #5: KINDNESS

KINDNESS is the perfect spiritual weapon to use for increasing prosperity. Being kind with your finances mean being gentle with responses towards bills and taking great care with your savings.

God has shown you so such mercy and kindness. He has blessed you even though you disobeyed his laws about giving and sharing. Many refuse to help their parents and friends who lack God's economic principles, yet, he still shows kindness by providing food and shelter for them indefinitely. There are many ways that God has shown kindness to you already. Look at your present job situation and the favor God has allowed to come to you through your co-workers and your boss.

All the education in this world cannot produce God's financial favor with others. It was God's perfect kindness that whispered in your boss's ear to let him/her know you were perfect for the job. While others are losing their jobs, you end up getting a promotion and a raise. While others are losing their homes, your mortgage is paid.

God has shown kindness by forgiving many even though they do not forgive others for the debts committed against them. What a mighty and powerful God we serve. One of the reasons why God is so kind to many is to provide unlimited opportunities allowing them to turn from their sinful ways and disobedience, so that he can love them the way he intended. God's desire for you is to prosper in all things, not to experience defeat.

Sowing seeds of kindness is an excellent way to position yourself to receive God's kindness. Show kindness by taking a friend out for dinner and paying for it or buy groceries for a friend who just lost his/her job. There are so many examples of how to sow seeds of kindness. This pleases God and prepares you to receive victory with your own financial battles.

Remember, in order to receive kindness with your finances, you must first show kindness to those who are struggling around you financially. Take a step of faith and create a list of those around you who may need your support. Begin showing kindness to each one and watch the financial miracles that will begin to happen for you and your household. You will end up with a harvest so large; you will not be able to consume it in this lifetime.

Examples how to apply the spiritual weapon of kindness:

1. Share this book with a friend.
2. Pay the grocery bill for the person in line ahead of you.
3. Buy lunch for all your co-workers.
4. Take someone without transportation to church in the car God blessed you with.
5. Send $20 cash to friends and relatives expressing God's love.
6. Pray for your neighbors to receive financial increase from God.
7. Invite a friend to share dinner with your family each month.

One day David asked, "Is anyone in Saul's family still alive-anyone to whom I can show kindness for Jonathan's sake?" **2 Samuel 9:1**

SMART AMMO #6: GOODNESS

GOODNESS is an essential spiritual weapon to use for confirming dominance. The same God who is all-powerful is the same God who is good and wise. His goodness far outgrows your capacity to contain. God has bestowed special blessings for those who use this weapon proudly.

There is no goodness without the Almighty God. It is surely impossible to separate that which is good from God. Many hope that God chooses them as one of his vessels to receive some of his goodness. God will withhold no good thing from you if you do what is right.

Others take for granted the jobs they have and the ability to increase savings. Then there are those who become so arrogant yet, God continues to show his goodness no matter how rebellious they become.

God is the only source of everything that is good. There is no need to look elsewhere. Everything that is good in your life comes from the one and true source Jehovah Jireh-The Lord Your Provider.

There are many who invest money into things that are not blessed by God, but God without a doubt will rescue them from every financial mistake. This is why you must believe with your heart that God will not allow any financial disaster to come to your home.

Most families can trace their unhappiness with their finances back to robbing God of the tithe. Anytime you find yourself struggling with your finances there is a high possibility that you or someone in your household has offended God financially.

Offending God financially releases an automatic stronghold into your life designed to rob you of 100% of your income because you refused to be obedient with ten percent. Refuse to be defeated in your finances and open up your heart and allow God to show you just how precious you are to him. God's goodness is unlimited and bountiful for all those who obey his financial laws.

Examples how to apply the spiritual weapon of goodness:
1. Be sincere about becoming financially responsible.
2. Expect to be blessed in all things.
3. Become what God intended you to be; prosperous and in good health.
4. Be a blessing to others.
5. Speak only good words about your finances.
6. Know goodness will follow all those who trust and believe in God.
7. Seek godly counsel before investing.

How great is the goodness you have stored up for those who fear you. You lavish it on those who come to you for protection, blessing them before the watching world.

Psalm 31: 19

SMART AMMO #7: FAITHFULNESS

FAITHFULNESS is an intelligent spiritual weapon that should be used to subdue and secure more income. Being faithful in obeying God's laws will produce success in all that you do. Everything you touch will prosper!

Reading and listening to the Word of God faithfully on a daily basis is a prerequisite for achieving prosperity. The bible is the only book on this planet that gives clear instructions, detailed information and an action plan on how to achieve success and wealth. Guaranteed!

In the business world our word is no longer our bond. Within our own families infidelity is now the norm. How refreshing it is to know that there is one among us who never cheats and never lies. His name is Jesus Christ.

Faithfulness hinges upon what you value as important. You stay committed and devoted only to the things you value. If you do not see how reading and listening to the bible daily could be valuable towards producing financial independence, it's safe to say you will not be faithful with the assignments listed in this book.

In all of God's relations with his children, he is faithful and his promises are true. You never need to worry about tomorrow because God's faithfulness and promises to bless you will always stand. You will never see a child of God abandoned or begging for bread. God's faithfulness takes great care of those who believe that he is their shepherd.

Faithfulness takes discipline and dedication. You cannot achieve financial independence while being unfaithful to the people God assigns to your life for greater good. Learn to value people, your job and all financial goals so that you can experience God's faithfulness in the middle of the storm.

At times many lose faith and believe that God will not provide for their homes just like he said he would. Many turn their backs on the scriptures. Others seek out financial strongholds for comfort. Let me assure you, God is also faithful in punishing his children when they disobey him.

Examples how to apply the spiritual weapon of faithfulness:
1. Practice being faithful regarding all financial arrangements.
2. Cherish the people God assigns to your life.
3. Hold the Word of God very close to every financial transaction.
4. Be very clear as to how God promised to bless you financially.
5. Cry out to God when tempted to spend his money irresponsibly.
6. Believe God will bring grace to your finances.
7. Testify to others about God's faithfulness in your finances.

Study this book of instruction continually. Meditate on it day and night so that you will be sure to obey everything written in it. Only then will you prosper and succeed in all you do. **Joshua 1:8**

SMART AMMO #8: GENTLENESS

GENTLENESS is a brilliant spiritual weapon that should be used for developing the character of compassion during financial warfare. We live in a world today where the spirit of anger replaces the spirit of gentleness. Tenderness is no longer a value or quality in our character.

There are those who constantly scream, cry and covet for bigger homes, faster cars and more credit. The spirit of gentleness is nowhere to be found in the lives of those who experience the financial stressors that come in acquiring the fast life.

Gentleness is mercy. It is in applying gentleness to your financial goals that you acquire victory. Gentleness lends a kind ear to others especially in a time of need. Replenishing the needs of others is a goal for those with the character of gentleness. By meeting the needs of others, God will meet your needs. The act of gentleness is a mandatory character to develop in order to experience financial independence.

Gentleness is an attribute which should be used successfully over and over again to manage financial statements and receipts more peacefully. There is no need to get angry when it comes time to do your taxes. Arm yourself with the smart ammo's listed in this chapter and use the spirit of gentleness to handle your financial situations triumphantly.

The supernatural strength that God gives comes with restraint and control. It is with gentleness that you will have the ability to control the inheritance of riches from the giver of life, Jesus Christ. Gentleness teaches how to be more considerate with financial adversities.

Operating in the spirit of gentleness is the same as operating in strength. It is when you are weak in your own strength that God gives supernatural power to deal with each financial woe. You must not fight this war in the flesh. I repeat, do not fight your financial wars in the flesh. Financial battles can only be won by skillfully using spiritual weaponry. Learn to lean on God. You are never alone during a financial crisis. God is always near. Be gentle with yourself and call on God's amazing power for direction.

Examples how to apply the spiritual weapon of gentleness:
1. Apply control when using of your credit cards.
2. Restrain from spending more than you earn.
3. Have compassion for those who are financially weak.
4. Help a friend with preparing a family budget.
5. Forgive the debt of someone who owes you money.
6. Be gentle with your financial authorities.
7. Fall on your knees and give God thanks for all those who bless you financially.

But the wisdom from above is first of all pure. It is also peace loving, gently at all times, and willing to yield to others. It is full of mercy and good deeds. It shows no favoritism and is always sincere. **James 3:17**

SMART AMMO #9: SELF-CONTROL

SELF-CONTROL is the appropriate spiritual weapon to use for mastering your financial choices. Self-control begins with the mastering of your thoughts. If you are unable to control what you think, you cannot control what you do. It is your thinking that determines who you are and who you will become financially in the future.

Self-control is accepting the reality that you cannot force your boss to give you a raise. However, you have the power to improve work ethics and effectiveness so as to attract increase. Personal improvement increases economic value.

Whether you have a $1 in your pocket or $1000 in your savings account, it will take self-control to manage both successfully. Everyone is responsible for the amount of daily increase or lack that they produce.

Self-control is accepting responsibility for your behavior so as to be in harmony with the Will of God. Your job is not your source, God is. You are capable of managing all increase effectively. People are not responsible for your financial success. You are!

This means asking God for wisdom and guidance with all spending. As you cooperate with the Will of God, self-control becomes a natural by-product. Whereby, showing evidence to the world that you are a true son or daughter of the Most High.

Without self-control, you cannot resist temptations to spend money foolishly.

Without self-control, you will fall prey to every financial scam. But because of Christ, you can become new, and therefore exhibit behaviors that are pleasing and acceptable in God's sight. Because of Christ, you can become successful in giving of the tithes and offerings. You are more than capable of bringing joy to your Heavenly Father; because you have been set free from financial bondage and sabotage through Christ.

Christ has already fought and won every financial battle for you. Stop acting like Jesus lost the war. God's children are not wimps. Your focus is to control your spending and give monies to the places that God chooses. The question is do you trust God enough to believe his Word.

Examples how to apply the spiritual weapon of self-control:

1. Become a master of your emotions.
2. Stay calm and repent every time you overspend.
3. Try to understand the reasons for over spending. (Are you medicating yourself?)
4. Think of all your financial misbehaviors as an opportunity for learning how to get closer to Christ.
5. Take action! Control all financial transactions.
6. Limit the use of credit cards or get rid of them.
7. Stay away from cash advance opportunities.

But the Holy Spirit produces this kind of fruit in our lives: love, joy, peace, patience, kindness, goodness, faithfulness, gentleness, and self-control. There is no law against these things. **Galatians 5: 22,233**

<u>Invitation Prayer to Receive Christ as Lord</u>

Dear God, I need you right now. I acknowledge that I have sinned against you by not trusting you to guide me with daily financial decisions. I thank you for sending Jesus Christ to die on the cross for my sins. I thank you Lord for your gift of mercy and forgiveness. I submit my soul to you completely. I commit my thoughts and behaviors to your will. Please come into my heart today as the Lord of my life. Fill me with the Holy Spirit as you promised in your Word that you would do if I asked in faith. I pray this prayer in Jesus Name.

Chapter Seven Summary: Spiritual Weaponry

SMART AMMO # 1 Love
The power of God's love brings unlimited favor. Creditors will not have a desire to reveal options for paying your bills without the favor of God.

SMART AMMO #2 Joy
Operating in joy towards your finances releases God's strength to increase financial opportunities and investments.

SMART AMMO #3 Peace
There is a peace that surpasses all understanding and it comes only from God. The spirit of peace can only enter your life when you pay your tithes and offerings.

SMART AMMO #4 Patience
Fight every financial battle until you win. Eternal patience is the ability to endure until victory has come. Do not back down without victory!

SMART AMMO #5 Kindness
It was God's perfect kindness that whispered in your boss's ear to let him/her know you were perfect for the job. God's kindness provides abundant resource for financial stability.

SMART AMMO #6 Goodness
The same God who is all powerful is the same God who is good and wise. God's goodness always outgrows your capacity to contain increase in wealth and riches.

SMART AMMO #7 Faithfulness
Faithfulness hinges upon what you value as important. Staying committed to being financially independent is a way of expressing faithfulness.

SMART AMMO #8 Gentleness
Gentleness lends a kind ear to others especially during the time of need. By meeting the needs of others, God will meet your needs according to his riches in glory.

SMART AMMO #9 Self-Control
Self-control is accepting responsibility for your thoughts and behavior so as to be in harmony with the Will of God. You are capable of managing your finances successfully. Your job is not your source, God is.

Chapter Seven: Voice Activated Financial Confessions

God has assured me that I will receive my financial harvest on time.

I am capable of managing my finances successfully.

Those who have stolen from me will pay back seven times what they have stolen.

I work hard for the Lord therefore my profit margins are very high.

God has surrounded me with many advisers. Therefore all my plans succeed.

I am surrounded with great wealth and luxury because God has made me wise.

Hasty shortcuts to financial success are no longer my desire.

I will not eat with people who are stingy and I will not desire their wealth.

My home is built by the wisdom of the True Living God.

I may fail financially seven times, but by the power of God in me, I shall be restored.

I am energetic, strong, and a hard worker.

God has increased my wealth, and yes, He is still the center of my life.

I am confident that my financial blessings come only from God.

Financial Prayer
Psalms 23

The Lord is my shepherd;
*   I have all that I need.*
He lets me rest in green meadows;
*   he leads me beside peaceful streams.*
*   he renews my strength.*
He guides me along right paths,
*   bringing honor to his name.*
Even when I walk
*   through the darkest valley,*
I will not be afraid,
*   for you are close beside me.*
Your rod and your staff
*   protect and comfort me.*
You prepare a feast for me.
*   in the presence of my enemies.*
You honor me by anointing my head with oil.
*   My cup overflows with blessings.*
Surely your goodness and unfailing love will purse me
*   all the days of my life,*
And I will live in the house of the Lord
*   forever.*

Be ready for war! Call out your best warriors. Let all your fighting men advance for the attack.

Joel 3:9

Chapter Eight

Offensive Warfare
(Sniper Tactics)

Chapter Eight: Offensive Warfare

Now that you have learned how to defend yourself properly during an attack, you must also learn how to develop offensive marksmanship skills to advance financially.

Those without their armor will say that it is impossible to advance financially. However, through reading the Bible, the Holy Spirit was able to give me a supernatural financial strategic plan that is easy to follow and has proven to be effective if used correctly.

It is mandatory that you implement an offensive economic strategic plan. Implementing an offensive strategic plan is about practicing skillful financial choices so as to produce stability and independence.

According to Genesis 25:34, Esau despised his birthright. To this day many of God's children continue to despise their birthright to multiply, bearing fruit, replenish, subdue, and take dominion. You cannot despise wealth and riches and expect financial increase.

Financial bondage is often a result of selling your birthright to strongholds for clothes bought on credit, houses you cannot afford and everything the lust of the flesh can imagine. You must refuse to dishonor the Alpha and the Omega. Pick up your bed and walk by implementing offensive economic strategies.

Offensive warfare enables you to claim new financial territory as you fight with dignity to share strategies with family members and friends; assisting them towards victory with their own financial war. As a child of the King, the goal is to hit the bulls-eye every time.

Staying on the offense during warfare is simply common sense. You must relentlessly pursue continuous financial improvement. Be proactive by using the sniper gears and tactics covered in this chapter over and over until you eliminate every financial hijacker attached to your wallet.

Establishing an offensive strategic economic plan is essentially a process of determining where you are currently, where you want to go financially, and how you plan to get there. This is not a race. There is no need to compete. Remember you are no longer a victim to financial strongholds.

Financial warfare is won through the following offensive strategies:

Step One: Become aware of your financial strengths by securing investments & savings.

Step Two: Declare financial war on every debt by preparing a plan of attack and wage war persistently until all debts are paid in full.

Step Three: Don't just work to pay your bills, look out for opportunities to increase your financial position to help others. Never leave the battlefield unattended.

Step Four: Stay on course by developing the ability to recognize a financial threat ahead of time.

Step Five: Be alert! It may sound like a good deal, but think what it will cost you and your family in a few years.

Step Six: Work hard at reflecting the nature of God by becoming financially responsible immediately.

God spoke: "Let us make human beings in our image, make them reflecting our nature so they can be responsible for the fish in the sea, the birds in the air, the cattle, and, yes, Earth itself, and every animal that moves on the face of the Earth." **Genesis 1:26**

Sniper Gears to Acquire for Offensive Warfare:

Sniper Gear #1: Multiply (Prosper)

Constant financial increase is a necessary ingredient needed to maintain a healthy and strong financial foundation. God's children are always prosperous and successful. There are no failures in Christ Jesus. God's children must assassinate their financial enemies and rise to a level of greatness that reflects their Heavenly Father's decree.

There are infinite products and ideas available that will produce capital for all those who persist. Everyone has the potential to create increase in their life. You are a direct reflection of the One who created you. You have the DNA of "The Christ".

God's children are confident, bold, and attract unlimited riches daily. No lack can live in your presence when you constantly look for ways to increase your wealth.

Take a strong financial position by creating multiple streams of income annually. Do not settle for the same financial increase annually. Inflation will not wait for you. Prices at the grocery stores, doctors and gas pumps are constantly increasing. Without yearly financial increase to off set this attack, you are consciously choosing to die. Embrace a financial offensive spirit and double your income potential by adding new sources of income quarterly or annually.

This would be a good time to invest in others with great ideas to improve the world. Try investing $100, $500, $1000 or more. Create several synergetic partnerships with the goal of increase in mind. You can invest for one or five years. Just do something!

Develop an economic plan with factors that display unlimited increase and refuse to live pay check to pay check. Multiplication does not support individuals who tolerate bondage, sabotage, strongholds or lack.

Multiplication can only reproduce after its kind. Those who live pay check to pay check cannot attract financial increase. An individual who tithes and saves a minimum of ten percent of every pay check has the potential to attract financial increase no matter the level of income. Try to increase your monthly savings by $10 or more. Push back the enemy by securing your savings.

God always think in multiplication. Just take a look around; how many diverse kinds of people do you see each day? How many amazing songs do you hear the birds singing in the mornings? How many different aromas can you smell from a beautiful flower? How many types of animals have you encountered in your life time? The list is endless, because God loves to multiply himself. The ability to multiply your finances comes from being good stewards with God's money. You are a good steward; therefore financial stability comes quickly to your home.

God blessed them: Prosper! Reproduce! Fill Earth! Take Charge! Be responsible for fish in the sea and birds in the air, for every living thing that moves on the face of the Earth. **Genesis 1:28**

You are capable of advancing financially in this war simply by expecting God's economic plan to work for your life. Give God a try. What are you afraid of? You have nothing to loose and much to gain, simply by putting God's principles to the test.

There should be physical evidence that you are advancing financially. You cannot advance in an offensive war with lack of capital. There are several sniper tools listed below to increase your ability to secure unlimited territory for the Lord (see the financial multiplication grid below).

Multiplication Grid

Direction:

Use the multiplication grid below to remind yourself of the different areas that multiplication must be achieved in order to become an effective offensive warrior. Feel free to add more areas upon successfully multiplying each attribute from this list. The goal is to keep advancing forward. Remember God is constantly multiplying himself on planet earth. Let's reflect back to God what brings him great joy; the art of his children advancing and prospering in this financial warfare through multiplication.

X	Tithes	Blessing Others	Success	Income	Ability to Increase	Abundance
Investments	Savings	Land	Stocks	Bonds	Mutual Funds	Product Ideas
Service Ideas	Integrity	Understanding	Wisdom	Offerings	Worship	Loyalty
Common Sense	Diligence	Fear of God	Knowledge	Love	Peace	Joy
Patience	Kindness	Goodness	Faithfulness	Gentleness	Self Control	Compassion
Time with God	Vision	Discernment	Good Judgment	Gratitude	Faith	Riches
Ownership	Testimony	Victories	Prayer	Winnings	Intelligence	Excellence

Take a long, hard look. See how great he is—infinite, greater than anything you could ever imagine or figure out! **Job 36:26**

Sniper Gear #2: Bear Fruit (Reproduce)

Financial success is the result of using your kingdom thinking to bear fruit. Bearing fruit requires energy and plenty of sleep. You must be in excellent physical condition to be able to keep up with the overflow that comes from successful synergistic partnerships.

Children of God who bear fruit are constantly paving the way for others. Take pride in producing more than enough so others around you can be blessed. Superior financial education will be necessary and vital at this stage to dismantle and force financial strongholds to back away from your family, your friends and your loved ones.

Lack should not be permitted to enter your home once you activate the offensive weapon of bearing fruit. Your responsibility is to become a financial resource to your family, your friend, and your community. You must develop timeless patience in securing the financial walls, gates, and atmosphere wherever you are stationed.

Bearing fruit with the intention of blessing others makes you highly potent and proficient. You are not infertile. You are a powerful and lethal weapon that produces new and innovative products, services and ideas that command the flow of abundance.

Soldiers who have gone through successful sniper training produce financial results that glories the same God that raised Jesus from the dead. These soldiers bring beautiful smiles to God's face daily. These soldiers are always volunteering to please God by positioning themselves as a strong financial leader in their community.

Several characteristics of soldiers who bear financial fruit with the intention of blessing others include:

1. High level of financial interdependence amongst others.
2. Committed to the financial success of others.
3. Willing to contribute finance generously.
4. Develops a relaxed atmosphere for decision making time.
5. Prepared to take financial risks.
6. Clear about financial goals and establishes deadlines.
7. Knows how to identify financial errors.
8. Has the capacity to create new and exciting ideas to produce more profit.
9. Get things done ahead of schedule.
10. Do not waste time.

Bearing financial fruit displays leadership, power and wisdom. The bible says that we will know who belong to God by the fruit they bear. Your God is an awesome God. Everything he creates is good and perfect. In addition, every financial adversity you experience, he will turn it around to make profit.

"Who told you that you were naked?" The Lord God asked. "Have you eaten from the tree whose fruit I commanded you not to eat?" **Genesis 3:11**

The God you serve is patient, and will not hesitate to correct you when you do not follow his lead. A perfect example of God's ability to reproduce successfully is Bishop T. D. Jakes. Bishop Jakes displays kingdom attributes for all to see that God will not withhold any good thing from those who do what is right. To learn more about this mighty man of God's accomplishments with his family, his friends and his community visit www.thepottershouse.com.

In order to bear fruit you must first plant seeds that are financially related in order to become abundantly wealthy. You cannot plant seeds of apples, oranges and bananas expecting a financial return.

Planting apple seeds will only produce apples. Planting a financial seed will produce a supernatural financial increase that yields a high profit. In addition, the Lord repays everyone who plants a financial seed into the lives of widows, orphans and the poor.

When a financial warrior bears fruit their investments leads to an economic growth that reproduces itself several times over. This is an example of kingdom living.

You can increase financial productivity by:
1. Honoring the value of your time.
2. Avoiding interruptions.
3. Establishing an hour of creation time daily.
4. Eating healthy, exercising and getting quality sleep.
5. Thanking God for financial wisdom and anointing.
5. Talking with optimistic people.
6. Constantly reviewing plans for short and long term financial goals.
7. Partnering with individuals with the same goal of bearing financial fruit for the benefit of others.

Financial warriors under normal circumstances reproduce in all seasons. There are no droughts. Excess is always available to match inflation. There are no surprise financial attacks or kidnapping for those who bear financial fruit indefinitely.

However, there are some who produce few fruits and suffer greatly during times of financial hardship and those who reproduce too quickly because of haste; ultimately they lose their homes, families and everything they have accomplished during their life time.

Then there is another level where many choose not to read financial books or select a financial mentor who can assist with creating a financial roadmap. These weak believers display a negative picture about God to people of this world, and will not survive or stand a chance at winning this financial war until they submit to God's economic plan. Bearing financial fruit is an assignment for all of God's children, not just those who pray and pay tithes.

But you belong to God, my dear children. You have already won a victory over those people, because the Spirit who lives in you is greater than the spirit who lives in the world. 1 John 4:4

Sniper Gear #3: Replenish (Fill Earth)

Replenishing your finances means to fill up your financial reserves. You must prepare for future challenges. Do not leave room for a financial hostage situation to take place.

Advancing on the offense directly commands that financial reserves be a necessary strategy to activate in order to accomplish dominion in the earth.

You can increase your financial reserves through diligent planning and expense management. Excellent financial reports can be kept by tracking the amount spent on necessary and unnecessary items such as; food, housing, entertainment, savings, shoes or eating out annually.

Most of your expenses are not necessary and if the same amount of money is managed well, it could yield millions of dollars if invested over a long period of time.

In order to replenish with power, you must first be tested. Every financial test means that it's time for inspection. This is not the time to file a complaint. It's time to make sure that your armor and spiritual weaponry are ready for immediate activation. You are more than capable of operating and managing several savings accounts effectively to eradicate debt. Remember you are a powerful spiritual weapon in the earth.

Establishing a strong financial reserve will prepare you to reinvest so as to maintain a position of financial strength. Spending $5 per day for coffee will cost you $150 per month, $1800 for one year, and $9,000 for five years. Just imagine investing $9,000 with compound interest, its mind numbing!

Now imagine investing more than $5 per day for twenty, thirty, forty or fifty years. You must cultivate a saving and investing mentality in order to maintain a level of performance that fully replenishes financial reserves millions of times over.

Financial inspections occur to see if you have mastered basic financial trainings covered in chapter three of this book. No longer will the body of Christ tolerate a financial slavery mentality. You must take your position immediately and learn how to implement God's economic plans that build generational wealth. It is necessary for you to become a successful steward of great wealth without delay. Advance to the frontline in Jesus Name.

Mark well that God doesn't miss a move you make; he's aware of every step you take. The shadow of your sin will overtake you; you'll find yourself stumbling all over yourself in the dark. Death is the reward of an undisciplined life; your foolish decisions trap you in a dead end. **Proverbs 5:21-23**

Establishing a financial endowment is an excellent way to replenish your community. A financial endowment is a transfer of money or property donated to an institution, with the stipulation that it be invested and the principle remains intact.

Securing an endowment fund for your community allows for your donations to have a much greater impact over a longer period of time than if it were spent all at once. This would be a great gift to leave to your church. However, many pastors refuse to teach financial management skills to its members, so many churches experience debt and foreclosures just like the world.

Why do we keep making the same mistakes? Why is there a church on every corner like McDonalds? Is there an operational and visionary plan for each church location? Why are church leaders in debt? Who owns the land that your church sits on? Can pastors who are in debt lead their people towards financial independence?

Don't you realize that we serve ONE GOD? Whose credit is being used to open new churches daily? Why aren't pastors partnering to reduce the burdens on their members? Why is it necessary to have a building fund for years at a time?

Where can church members get assistance with their financial pain? Why do pastors take so many offerings in one service? Where is the money coming from? Is it coming from the financially illiterate?

You cannot move to this offensive level financially by taking advantage of individuals who lack financial education. You are creating financial curses on your family if you continue to steal from individuals who trust you.

As a financial warrior it is your responsibility to seek financial wisdom so crooks and thieves will not use your money to build bigger homes for themselves, while you sit by and watch your family commit suicide due to high levels of financial stress.

Your assignment is to occupy the earth until God returns. Stop advancing to a consumer, victim mentality and begin replenishing your financial reserves today.

Let my enemies be destroyed by the very evil they have planned for me.
Psalm 140: 9

Sniper Gear #4: Subdue (Take Charge)

Subdue means to conquer and bring into subjection. You cannot subdue your finances by withholding the tithe. The tithe is a pre-requisite before the offensive sniper gear of subduing can work. Once the tithe is released to your spiritual teacher, advance patiently to the following sectors:

1. Savings (10% of all income)
2. Credit Card Debt (Include department stores)-**PAID IN FULL**
3. Automobile Debt-**PAID IN FULL**
4. Mortgage Debt-**PAID IN FULL**
5. Investments (Increase annually)

Pay close attention to emotional spending. Do not shop without a list. Purchase items on sale that is already scheduled in your monthly budget. Negotiate right down to the penny. Never purchase an item at full price. When new items present themselves for purchase, resist temptation and bring this new purchase under subjection by writing a note for that purchase to be reviewed before next month's budget.

Subdue the thoughts being created about your financial destination. Monitor the language being used to describe your ability to advance financially. Arrest every negative thought that tells you "You cannot follow this plan" or "It does not work."

Do not welcome thoughts that defeat your ability to become successful. Do not read, listen or speak with anyone that promotes a message of how to become a financial failure. Resist all financial strongholds and arm yourself with God's power, intelligence, and unlimited resources to conquer all enemies without hesitation.

The art of using the offensive sniper gear of subduing brings lasting financial increase. The goal in any war is to control the enemy and you are more than qualified.

All financial strongholds must be brought into subjection one at a time. Leave no room for re-entry. Secure your position as a warrior and leave no enemy alive. Eliminate every kind of spending that threatens your ability to live in great wealth and prosperity.

Take the necessary steps to become debt free. Evaluate your performance daily or weekly in order to maintain your leadership status. Increase financial strategic planning sessions and reduce time wasting activities such as television, the phone, and the internet.

You cannot subdue a financial enemy by investing forty hours weekly watching television and investing less than an hour each week for financial planning.

You have armed me with strength for the battle; you have subdued my enemies under my feet. **Psalm 18:39**

In addition, remember that you are not of this world and must invest quality time creating financial strategies from the Spirit realm in order to advance to the offensive warrior status.

Stand firm by building financial security for your children's children. Control your selfishness by establishing a trust and education fund for the next generation. Conquer all desires of your flesh to spend every penny and establish a retirement fund that takes care of your health at a later date.

Do not leave "Getting Older Care" or funeral bills for your children or grandchildren to pay. This action helps Satan to keep your family in financial bondage. Purchase life insurance ahead of time to help your family members pay for outrageous bills acquired before and after their burial. Subdue all financial strongholds or they will subdue you!

Overcome habits of repeating the same financial mistakes over and over again. Read this book one hundred times if needed until every secret, defensive and offensive weapon, is attached to your spirit. Learn to live, sleep, and think of ways to advance financially for the betterment of yourself, your family and your community.

Staying on the financial offense is mandatory. Hold your head high knowing that the God you serve has given you complete victory during this financial war. Be the first to establish a successful economic plan for your family.

Force creditors to change their strategy towards you by taking responsibility with all bills. Strengthen your current financial position by refusing to go further into debt. Formulate financial plans that force every enemy to retreat off your property, your bank accounts, and all possessions.

No enemy has the right or authority to steal your inheritance. Blessings are stolen due to your inability to believe God's Word. Without faith in the Word of God, you cannot access the power and authority to speak to things as if they were. Learn to trust in a God that fights for his children.

Who can snatch the plunder of war from the hands of a warrior? Who can demand that a tyrant let his captives go? But the Lord says, "The captives of warriors will be released, and the plunder of tyrants will be retrieved. For I will fight those who fight you, and I will save your children. **Isaiah 49: 24,25**

<u>Sniper Gear # 5: Dominion (Be Responsible)</u>

The ultimate mission of every financial warrior is to become a world leading supplier and lender. Learn to concentrate your efforts on becoming a master of a financial destination that serves others. Design superior products and provide excellent services until you become a master in that industry.

God did not command you to work a 9 to 5 job, pay bills and die early. In Genesis, God made it very clear for you to take dominion in the earth. This means being responsible with the things God placed into your hands. Acquiring financial dominion is an offensive weapon that produces a surplus that looks after three or four generations, not just the present.

Financial warriors who make it to this level are confident and optimistic about their financial future. Negative thinking and doubt are not ingredients of an individual who seek to acquire this weapon.

At this level take advantage of opportunities and invest a large part of your high disposable income for the long-run. Try to acquire several small businesses. Follow an economic plan that **reduces** spending and seek wise counsel. Believe for your success level to grow to infinite possibilities.

Global investing is usually on the mind of a financial warrior who respects God's command of taking dominion. Another goal is to dominate in the east, west, north and south. Financial expansion is a necessary step to confuse strongholds.

There are many families with aunts, uncles, cousins, brothers and sisters without jobs. Many of these family members live in other parts of the world. Use your intelligent discernment and create business opportunities for each family member. Increase your position and expand financially by helping others.

You are called to dominate financially, not to be good little consumers. Manage your wealth with passion. Tolerate more risk and earn higher returns.

Never forget the God who gives you the power to achieve success and create wealth. Identify clearly that it is "God" who made you rich for his glory.

Seek the Lord in the mornings to fill your homes with prosperity and peace. Train your children to invest at an early age so as to secure higher compound interest. This is your time!

*I chased my enemies and caught them; I did not stop until they were conquered. I struck them down so they could not get up; they fell beneath my feet. **Psalm 18:37,38***

Practice dividing your investments among many places. Do not invest one hundred percent of your funds in a savings account that yields a one percent return. Download financial intelligence from all resources to make quality decisions that commands unlimited increase.

The object in war is to beat the enemy. Establishing a clear position that dominates economically should be your object. Your financial enemies must be stopped. Therefore, command all financial delays and setbacks to step down immediately from their post and release to you every financial blessing that belongs to you. Tell the devil to BACK OFF!

Embrace a strong desire to please God and invest in your choice of real estate and collectibles. Nothing is impossible for a warrior who has acquired the sniper gear of dominion.

God has given you complete financial authority to care for the poor, and experience great riches many generations over. No financial harm will come to those who do what is right. You must not retreat or hesitate. God is on your side, who dare come against a child of God?

Follow strict financial doctrines and principles as a foundation strategy to use daily in order to increase your ability to dominate. A clear example of one of God's children who has achieved this level of financial dominance is Joel Olsteen. To learn more about Joel's many accomplishments visit www.joelolsteen.lakewood.cc

Look, I have given you authority over all the power of the enemy, and you can walk among snakes and scorpions and crush them. Nothing will injure you. **Luke 10:19**

Example of a One Year Economic Battle Plan

Financial Vision:
Living abundantly, healthy, prosperously, and wealthy in a way that brings Glory to your Heavenly Father.

Financial Mission: Proverbs 3:9,10
Honor the Lord with your wealth and with the best part of everything you produce. Then he will fill your barns with grain, and your vats will overflow with good wine.

Financial Goals:
> **January:** Pay tithes-Leviticus 27:30
> **February**: Seek God for my children's financial blessings-Genesis 13:15
> **March**: Be courageous when finances are low-Luke 12:32
> **April**: Be faithful with what God gives me-Luke 16:10
> **May:** Give all to God-Exodus 22:29
> **June**: Sow seeds on good ground-Mark 4:20
> **July:** Ask God for help with finances-Psalm 2:8
> **August**: Give where the Lord chooses-Deuteronomy 14:8 & 9
> **September**: Stop being stingy-Proverbs 23:6 & 7
> **October**: Refuse to be lazy-Proverbs 26:16
> **November**: Obey all decrees and regulations of the Lord-1 Chronicles 22:13
> **December**: Feed God with my offerings-Deuteronomy 28

Strategies:
- Meet with a financial mentor monthly to review plans and budgets for gaining financial increase and independence.
- Partner with others to increase financial growth.
- Use tithes and offerings to secure financial boundaries.
- Spend one hour (minimum) weekly marketing personal talents and abilities to the community.
- Increase financial wisdom by participating in a weekly bible study.

Action Plan:
1. Prepare a Financial Picture Board for goals quarterly. (Visit local arts & crafts store for ideas and supplies)
2. Pray over Financial Picture Board daily.
3. Give God thanks for the physical manifestation of each financial goal.
4. Share testimony with ten people about what God has done.
5. Lead five new people to Jesus Christ with financial testimony.
6. Share this economic plan with others.
7. Declare daily: "Jesus rose from the dead and has already given me victory with all financial assignments and goals."
8. Save 10% of all income.

Example of an Offensive Economic Strategic Plan:

Phase One: (Multiply)
Tithe (10% of income)
Personal Savings Account (10% of income)
Debt Elimination Account (10% of income)
Money Market Checking Account
Retirement Account
Education Fund for Children
Household Budget Account (one month)
Annual Family Vacation Account
Small Business
Homeownership
Land Ownership
Life Insurance
Will

Phase Two: (Bear Fruit)
Tithe (15% of income)
Personal Savings Account (15% of income)
Emergency Account (one month income)
Household Budget Account (three months)
Trust Fund for Children
Disability Insurance
Stocks and Bonds
Mutual Funds
Synergistic Partnership with the Community
Personal Home (Debt Free Mortgage)

Phase Three: (Replenish)
Tithe (20% of income)
Personal Savings Account (20% of income)
Household Budget Account (six months)
Investment Properties

Phase Four: (Subdue)
Tithe (25% of income)
Personal Savings Account (25% of income)
Household Budget Account (nine months)
Global Investing
Lender to Community

Phase Five: (Dominion)
Tithe (30% of income)
Personal Savings Account (30% of income)
Household Budget Account (twelve months or more)
Family Foundation (providing a solution for the community)
Endowment

Chapter Eight: Offensive Warfare Summary

Sniper Gear #1 Multiply
Reflect the power of God's ability to multiply by creating multiple streams of income and savings annually.

Sniper Gear #2 Bear Fruit
Bear financial fruit by paving the way for others. Produce more than enough so others around you can be blessed.

Sniper Gear #3 Replenish
Replenish finances by filling up your financial reserves.

Sniper Gear #4 Subdue
Subdue all financial situations by controlling desires to overspend.

Sniper Gear #5 Dominion
Become a world leading supplier and lender. Concentrate all efforts on mastering a financial destination that serves others.

Chapter Eight: Voice Activated Financial Confessions

In God, I experience financial wisdom and knowledge.

I use the weapons of righteousness in my right hand for attack and my left hand for defense.

I devote myself to prayer with an alert mind and a thankful heart.

I am always joyful. I am thankful in all circumstance.

I am armed with the armor of God so I will be able to stand firm against all strategies of the devil.

I have received my inheritance from God.

God has chosen me in advanced, and he makes everything work out according to his plan.

My God is not a man, so he does not lie. Wealth and Riches belongs to me.

God is not human, so he does not change his mind. Victory over poverty and debt belongs to me.

I persist patiently until I succeed.

All my needs are met in Jesus Christ!

I am in constant need of God's leadership and guidance.

God has removed all poverty conscious behavior from me so I may bring more glory to him.

Adversity and goodness comes from the Lord, thank you Father for preparing me to receive both without complaining.

God has given me treasures hidden in the darkness-secret riches.

Financial Prayer
Genesis 32: 9,10

The Jacob prayed, "O God of my grandfather Abraham, and God of my father, Isaac-O Lord, you told me, 'Return to your own land and to your relatives. 'And you promised me, 'I will treat you kindly.' I am not worthy of all the unfailing love and faithfulness you have shown to me, your servant. When I left home and crossed the Jordan River, I owned nothing except a walking stick. Now my household fills two large camps!

So I run with purpose in every step. I am not just shadowboxing.

1 Corinthians 9:26

Victory Lap

Personal financial battles began heating up as I started to write chapters six, seven, and eight of **Financial Warfare**. Distractions multiplied to change the publication deadline. However, I was prepared and ready to defend the kingdom of God that lives within me. It's an awesome feeling to see how God's supernatural power works for my good.

People who owed me money from the past started paying me back. Checks came in the mail with love notes attached. One lady wrote in her card "God said to give you this." Inside was a check that brought a beautiful smile to my face. God is amazing!

God began showing off, and phone calls came from everywhere to create partnerships for more increase. Now understand; this is all happening before **Financial Warfare** reaches the publishing house. I felt my relationship with God had reached several dimensions.

The mere fact that you are reading this book is a clear sign that God is good to those who diligently seek him. There is no one else who can love and care for you like God. The same God that chose me to write this book is the same God waiting for you to say "YES" to him. Trust me, he will never fail you.

The experience of writing the **Financial Warfare** book prepared me to fall deeper in-love with God. My heart opened up to more people than I ever thought possible. Instead of thinking about myself; I started looking for new and exciting ways to help others become financially independent. Making sure that people around me had more than enough food and money for gas became a big priority. My personal financial situation and issues became secondary because God had gone ahead of me and made the crocked places straight. God's shield continues to cover and keep me safe and secure. I lack nothing!

The inability to use God's financial weapons skillfully in my twenties and thirties was the reason for outrageous debt and financial distress that followed my family for decades. Writing **Financial Warfare** allowed me to locate the root of my financial problems. It taught me how to implement the Word of God with power and confidence to receive the promises of God. In his arms I am protected. You will never fail, if you allow God to lead you. It is now your turn to be a Cyrus *(Isaiah 45)* to others.

May God Bless you with double the blessings he has in store for me. I release into your life the spirit of wealth, prosperity and generosity. I bind every financial stronghold attached to your inheritance and command that you live in a debt free home. I command all your needs met, you lack nothing, and you walk confidently knowing you are an heir to unlimited wealth and riches in Jesus Name. Amen!

I tell you the truth, until heaven and earth disappear, not even the smallest detail of God's law will disappear until its purpose is achieved.

Matthew 5:18

Warrior Resources

Books	Author
Called to Conquer	Bishop Eddie Long
Your Best Life Now	Joel Olsteen
Secrets of the Richest Man Who Ever Lived	Dr. Mike Murdock
Making Your Money Count	Kenneth Ulmer
The Millionaire Mind	Thomas Stanley
The Richest Man in Babylon	George Gleason
Kingdom Principles of Financial Increase	Dr. Nasir Siddiki
Speak the Word Over Your Family for Finances	Harry & Cheryl Salem
Financial Peace	David Ramsey
I Saw the Lord	Anne Graham Lotz
Rules of Engagement	Cindy Trimm
Your Credit Score	Liz Weston
Reposition Yourself	T.D. Jakes
Smart Couples Finish Rich	David Bach
The Principles and Power of Vision	Dr. Myles Munroe
Becoming a Millionaire God's Way	Dr. Thomas Anderson
Giving	Bill Clinton
The 250 Personal Finance Questions Everyone Should Ask	Peter Sander
The Science of Getting Rich	Wallace Wattles
Girl, Get Your Credit Straight	Glinda Bridgforth
Fight Like a Girl	Lisa Bevere
Healing is a Choice	Steve Arterburn
Battlefield of the Mind	Joyce Myers

CD's & DVD	Author
Start Smart Finish Rich	David Bach
One Minute Manager	Ken Blanchard
The Uncommon Millionaire	Dr. Mike Murdock
Financial Confessions	Yvonne Brooks
God's Creative Power for Financial Increase	Charles Capps
Turn Your Debt into Wealth	John Cummuta
Money is My Friend	Bishop David Evans
Strike 1, Strike 2, Strike 3, Satan You're Out	Dr. Jesse Duplantis
Real Estate Investor's College	Dolf De Roos'
Position Yourself to Prosper	Bishop T.D. Jakes
How to Receive from God	Kenneth Hagin
How to Build Wealth Like Warren Buffet	Robert Miles
Organizing from the Inside Out	Julie Morgenstern
The Six-Day Financial Makeover	Robert Pagliarini
The Next Millionaires	Phil Plizer
Financial Freedom	Anthony Robbins
The Art of Exceptional Living	Jim Rohn
You're Not Broke You Have A Seed	Dr. Leroy Thompson
Visu-Finance Bible Study	Yvonne Brooks
Maxed Out (Documentary)	James Scurlock

Remember, it is sin to know what you ought to do and then not do it.

James 4:17

About the Author

Author, teacher, and motivational speaker, Yvonne Brooks is the founder and director of the Brooks & Brooks Foundation, Inc., a non-profit organization that provides a series of leadership trainings online, after school and home study for children and parents throughout the United States and Worldwide.

Yvonne provides workshops, seminars, and specialized training programs in a variety of subjects. Yvonne is also the creator of the Teen Success Book Series, Visu-Finance Bible Study, Financial Boot Camp for Mothers and Daughters, Kids Financial Coaching and the Kids/Teens Investors Club available at elementary, middle and high schools.

All Scriptures is inspired by God and is useful to teach us what is true and to make us realize what is wrong in our lives. It corrects us when we are wrong and teaches us to do what is right. God uses it to prepare and equip his people to do every good work.

2 Timothy 3:16,17

Other Books and Products by Yvonne Brooks

Daily Financial Journal (Book)	$27.95
Visu-Finance Bible Study (DVD)	$19.99
Financial Confessions (CD)	$15.99
100 Ways to Become a Successful Teenager (Book)	$13.95
Financial Planning for Teens (Book)	$11.95
Visu-Success Pre-Teen Plan (DVD)	$19.99
Kids Success Journal (Book)	$26.95
Kids Finance 101(Book)	$17.95
Kids Success Calendar	$10.00
Kids Financial Intelligence (Flashcards)	$39.99
Kids Investment Portfolio Manager (Booklet)	FREE
Kids/Teens Investors Club Ages 5-18	Sponsored

For more information or to order:
Visit: www.youthleadership3000.org
Or
Call: 818-623-7332

There is so much more I want to tell you, but you can't bear it now.

John 16:12

WARNING:

Dirty Financial Secrets Exposed!

Financial Warfare is a remarkable book that has already helped many readers gain financial independence and success within months. No financial war can be won without powerful weaponry. Living paycheck to paycheck is no longer acceptable!

The book **Financial Warfare** is packed with incredible secrets on how to use financial weapons with skill and power. **Financial Warfare** exposes readers to the dangers of the top fifteen financial strongholds and the pickpocket tactics they use to steal money from the financially illiterate and the working poor.

Financial Warfare Reveals Strategies on How to:
- Prepare for Financial Combat
- Identify Financial Threats Ahead of Time
- Battle Successfully Against Financial Strongholds
- Defend and Subdue Financial Enemies
- Move Offensively Towards Financial Stability

Financial Warfare reveals some of the most extensive weaponry necessary to create increase and take financial territory immediately. The treasure of darkness and secret riches is already released. There is only first place in this war. Thus **Financial Warfare** is a prerequisite for becoming a warrior that wins financial battles every time!

Though the cherry trees don't blossom and the strawberries don't ripen, though the apples are worm-eaten and the wheat fields stunted, though the sheep pens are sheepless and the cattle barns empty, I'm singing joyful praise to God. I am turning cartwheels of joy to my Savior God. Counting on God's Rule to prevail, I take heart and gain strength. I run like a deer. I feel like I'm king of the mountain! **Habakkuk 3:17-19**

Yvonne Brooks is an educator and mentor for families nationwide. She lives happily in California with her family.

978-0-595-51892-0
0-595-51892-3

Printed in the United States
134940LV00001B/275/P